Angela Porter's
Zen Doodle Designs

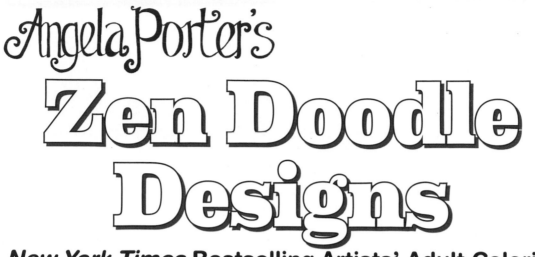

Angela Porter's Zen Doodle Designs

New York Times Bestselling Artists' Adult Coloring Books

ANGELA PORTER

Racehorse Publishing

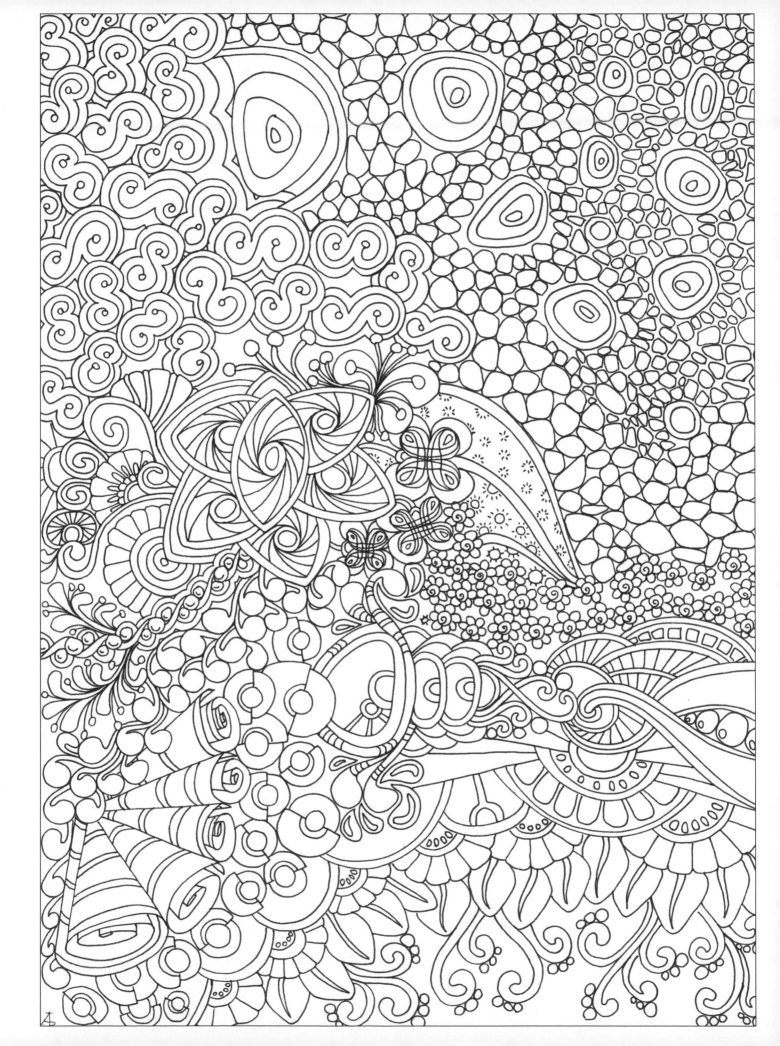

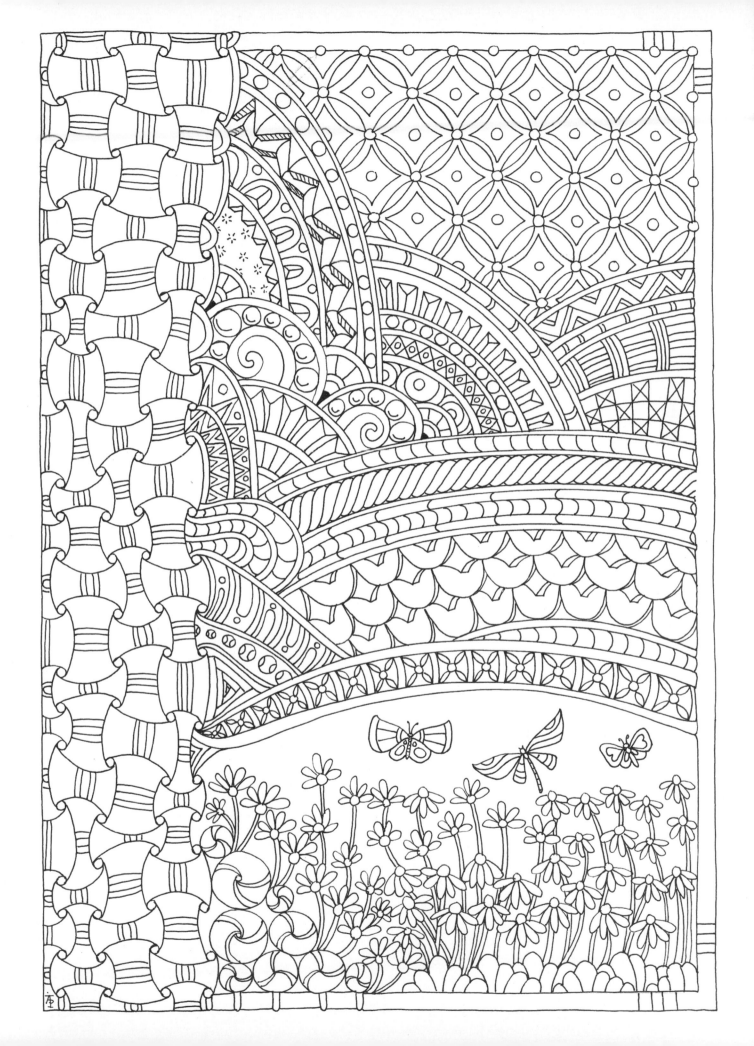

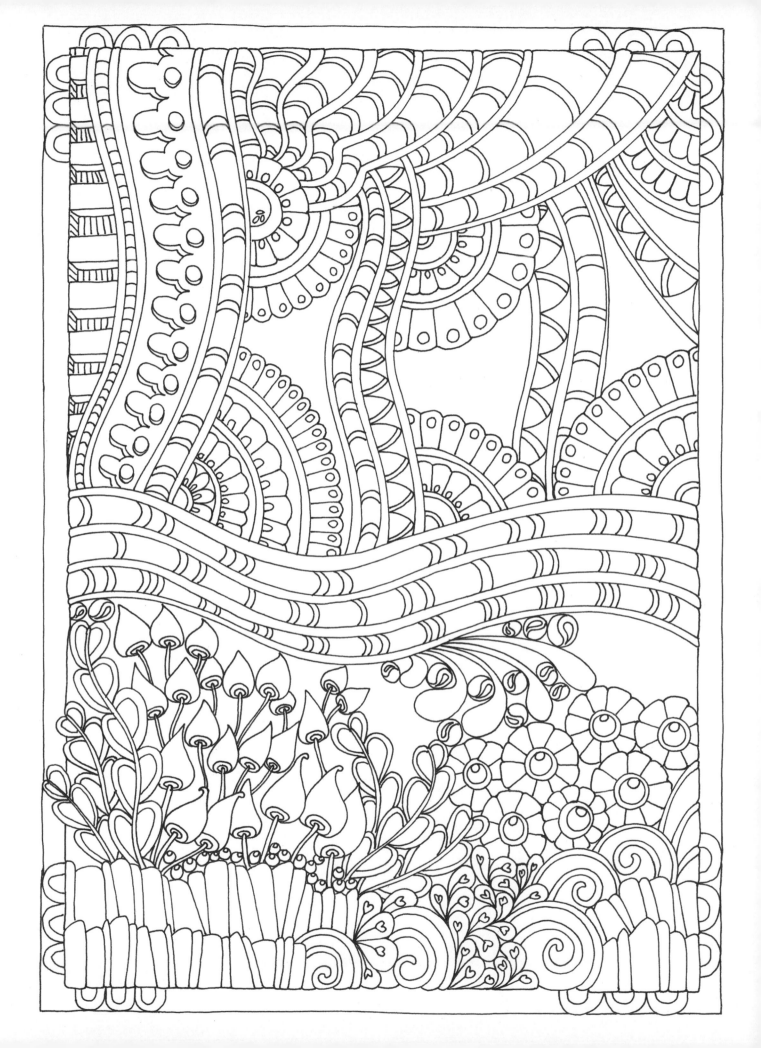

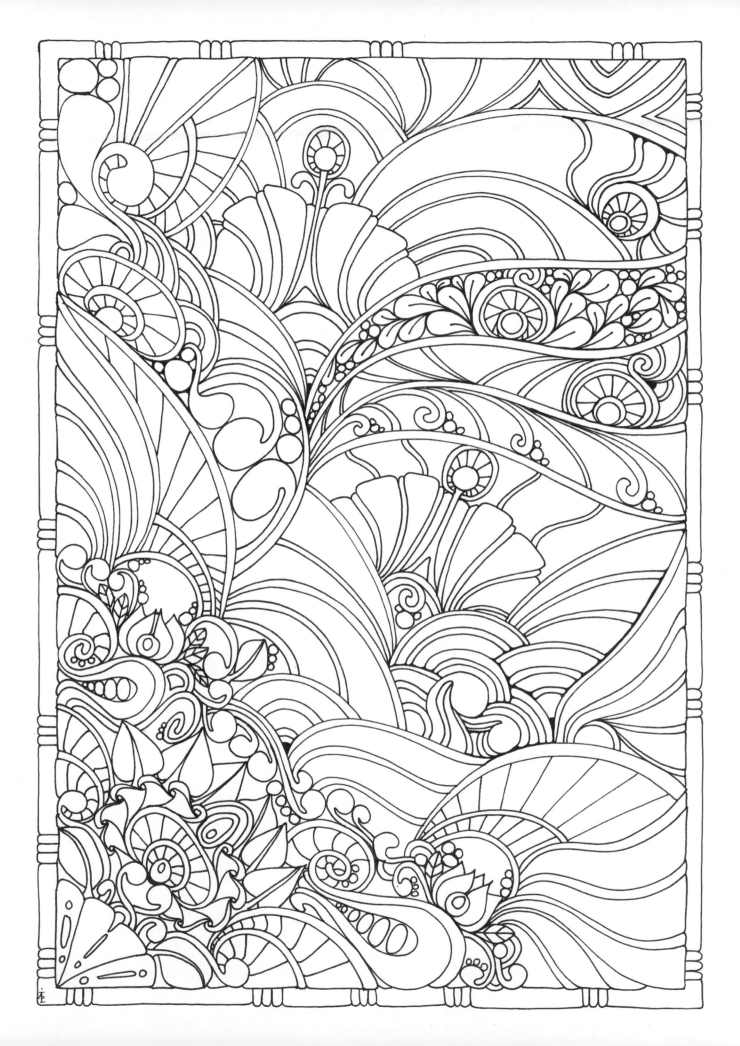

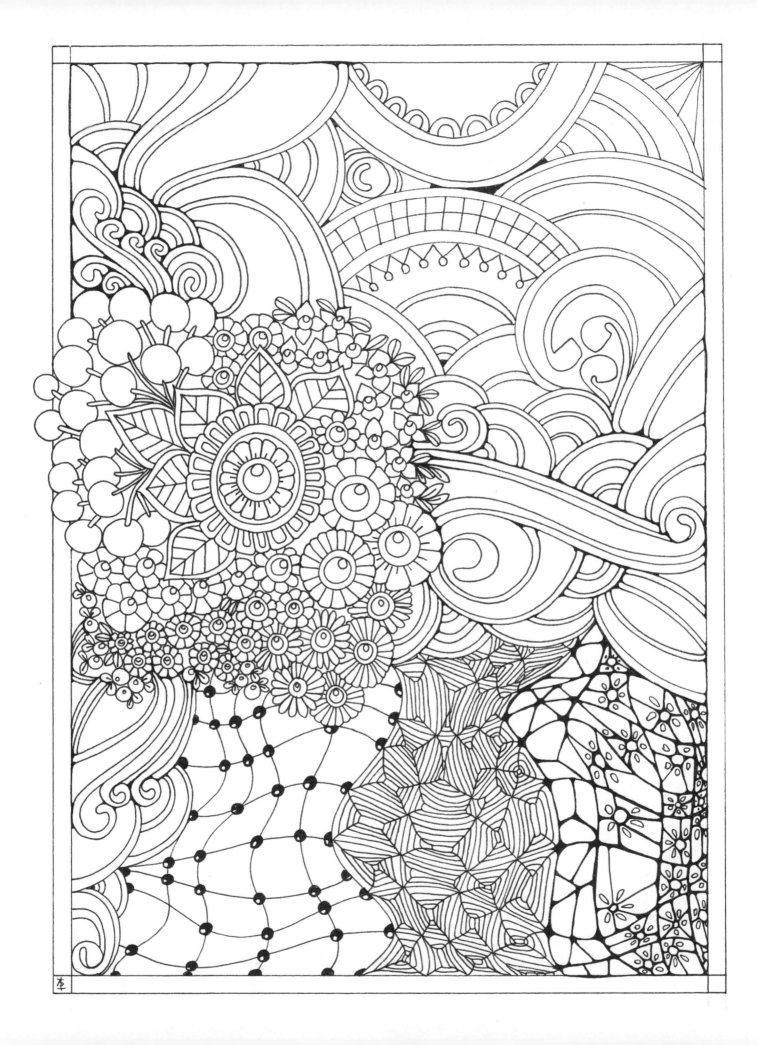

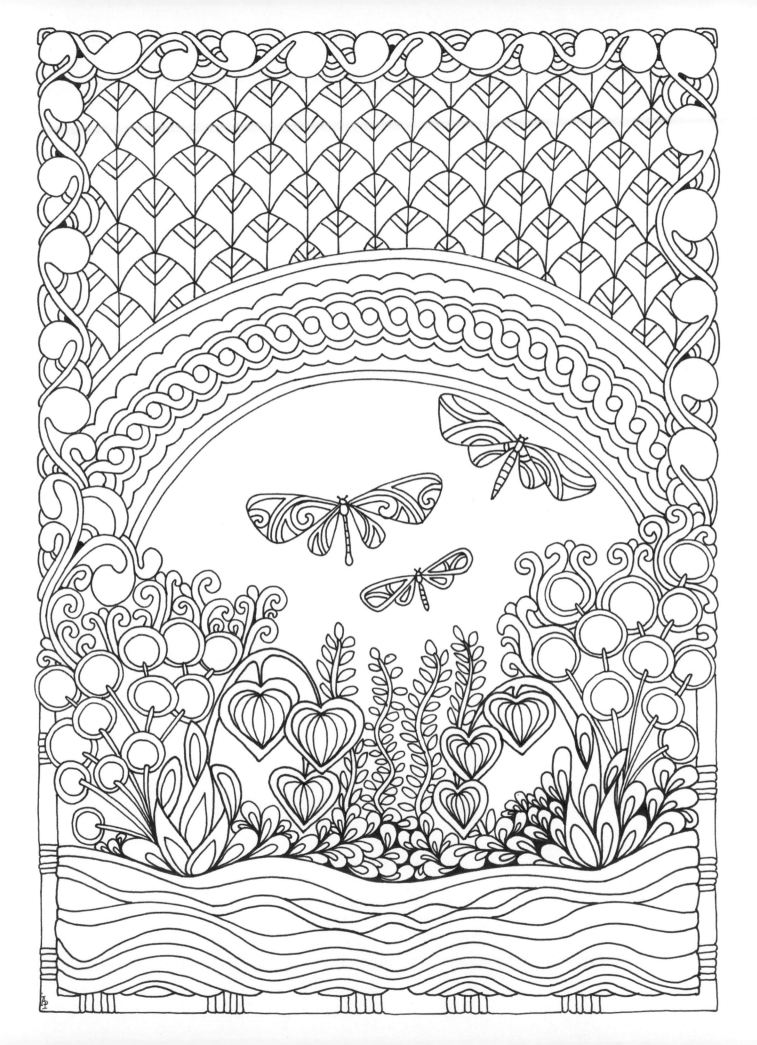

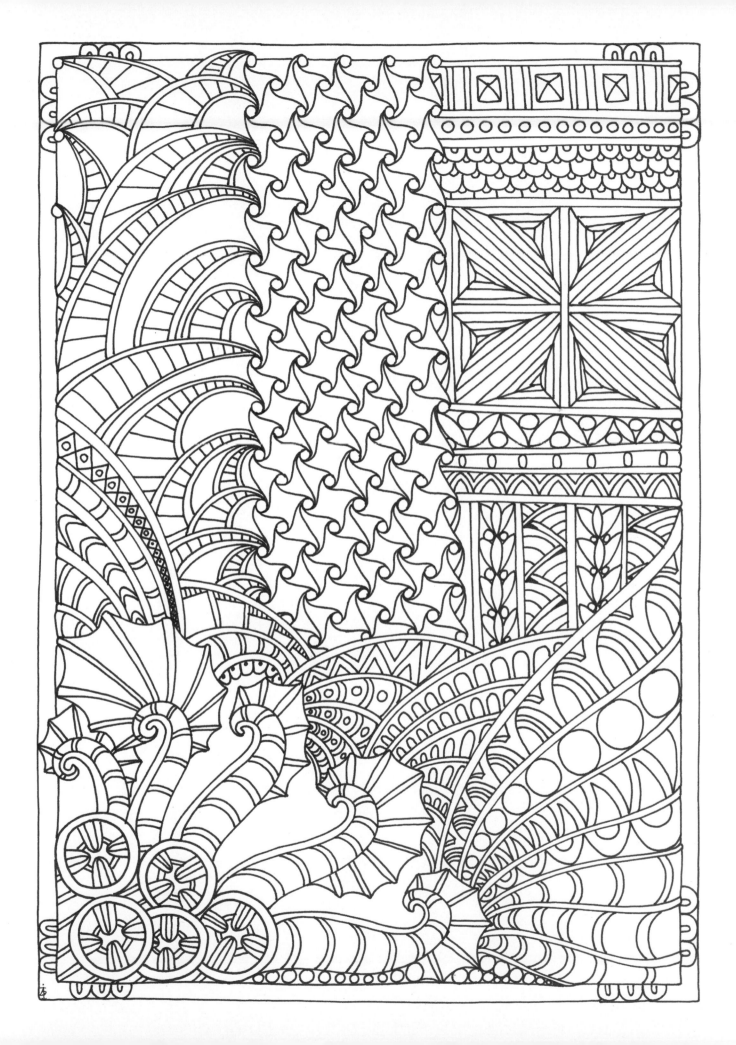

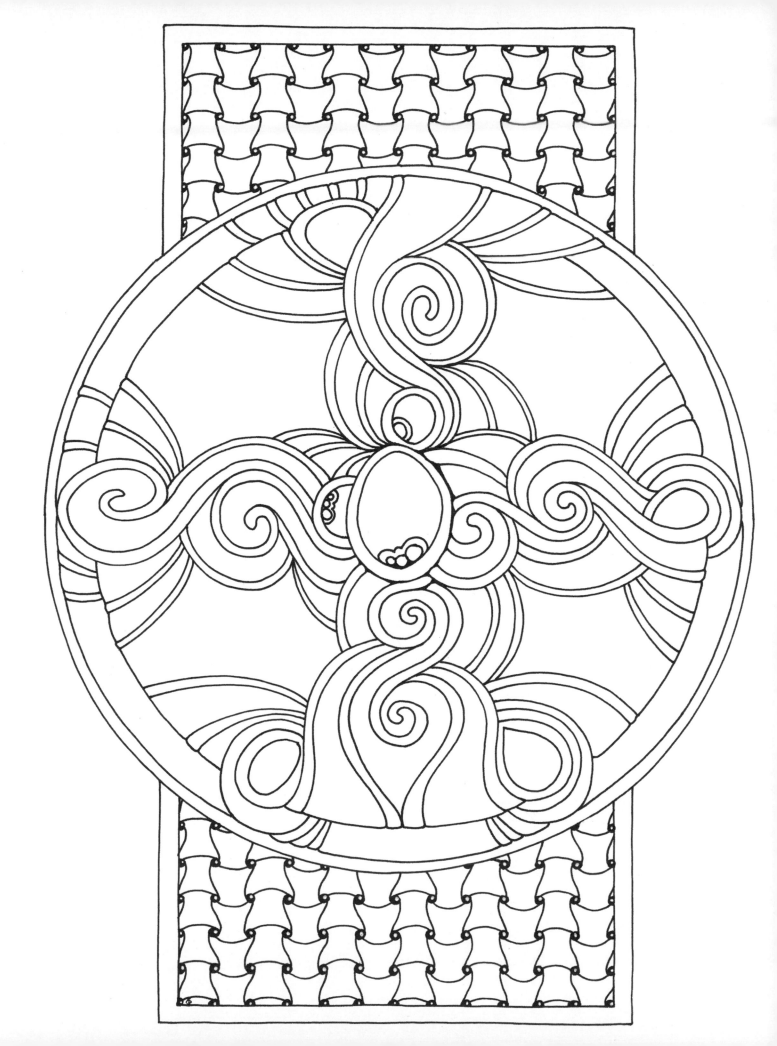

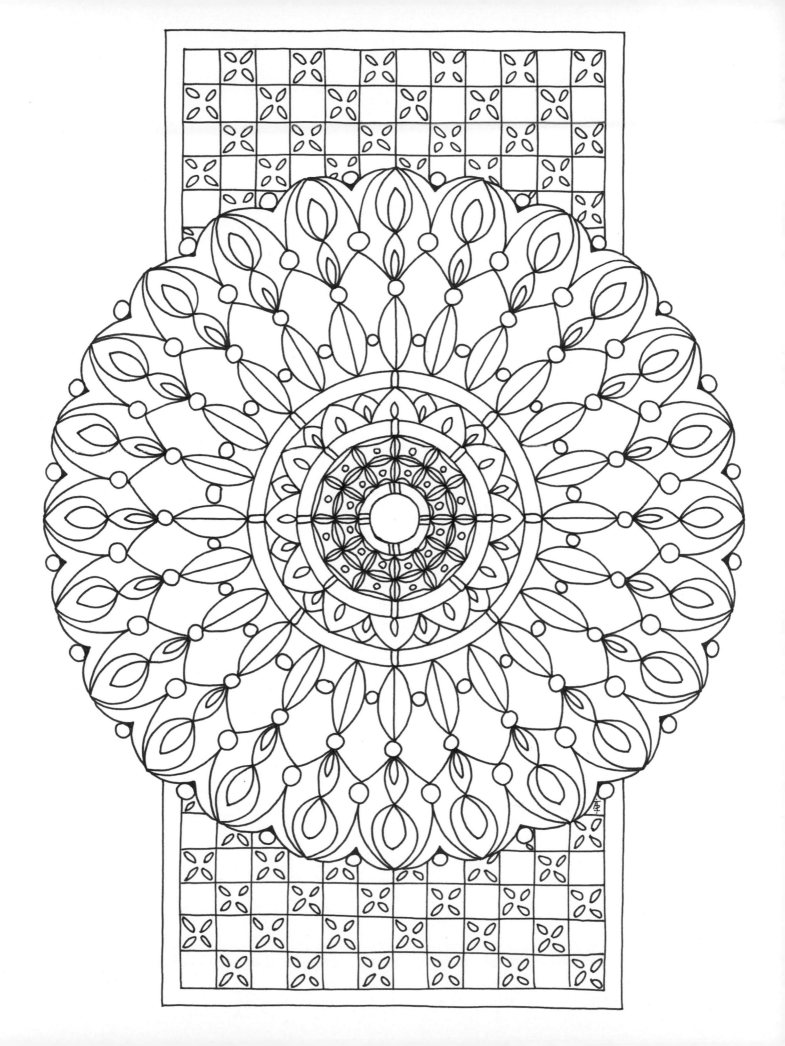

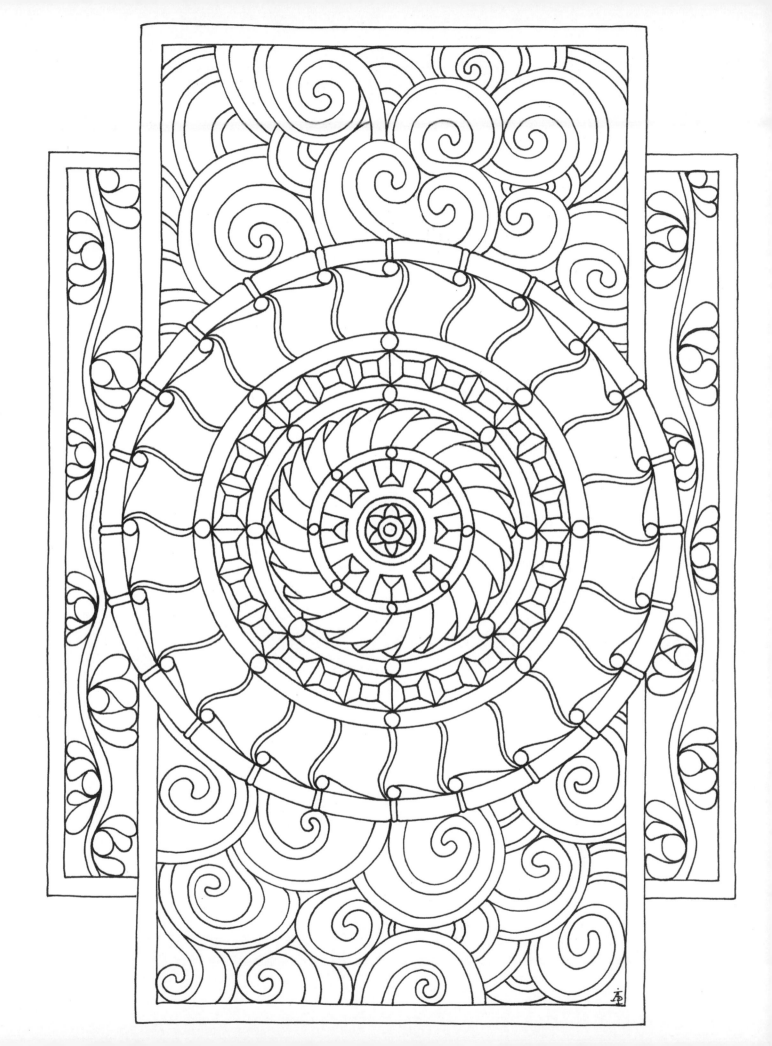

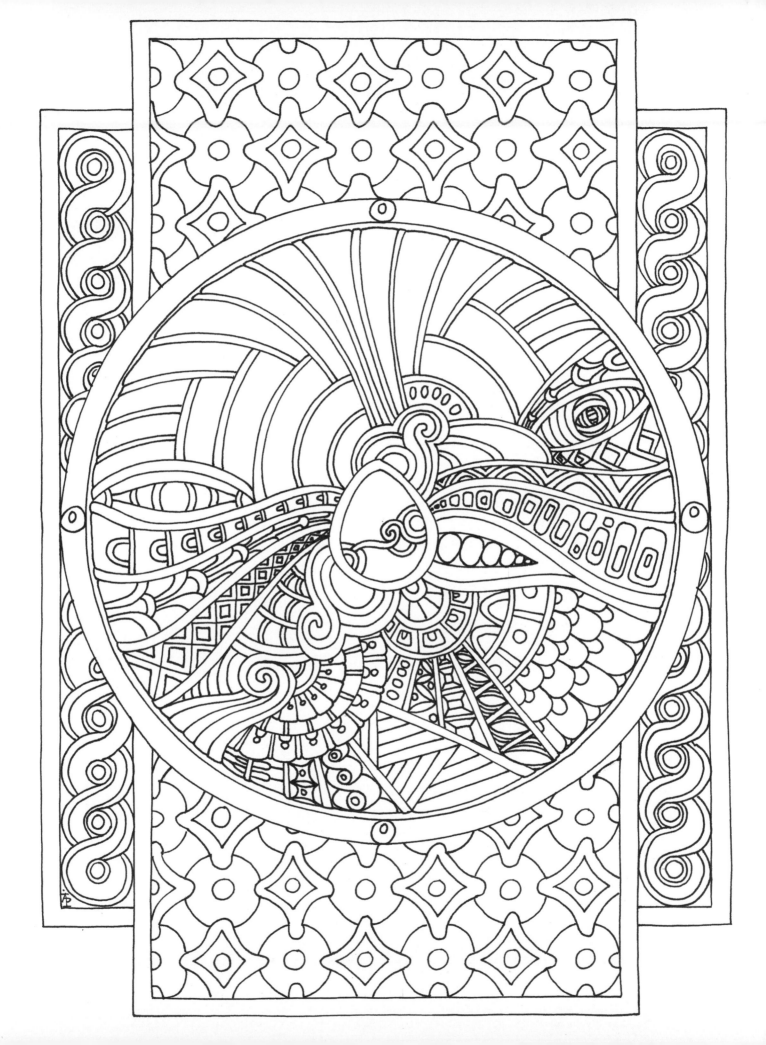

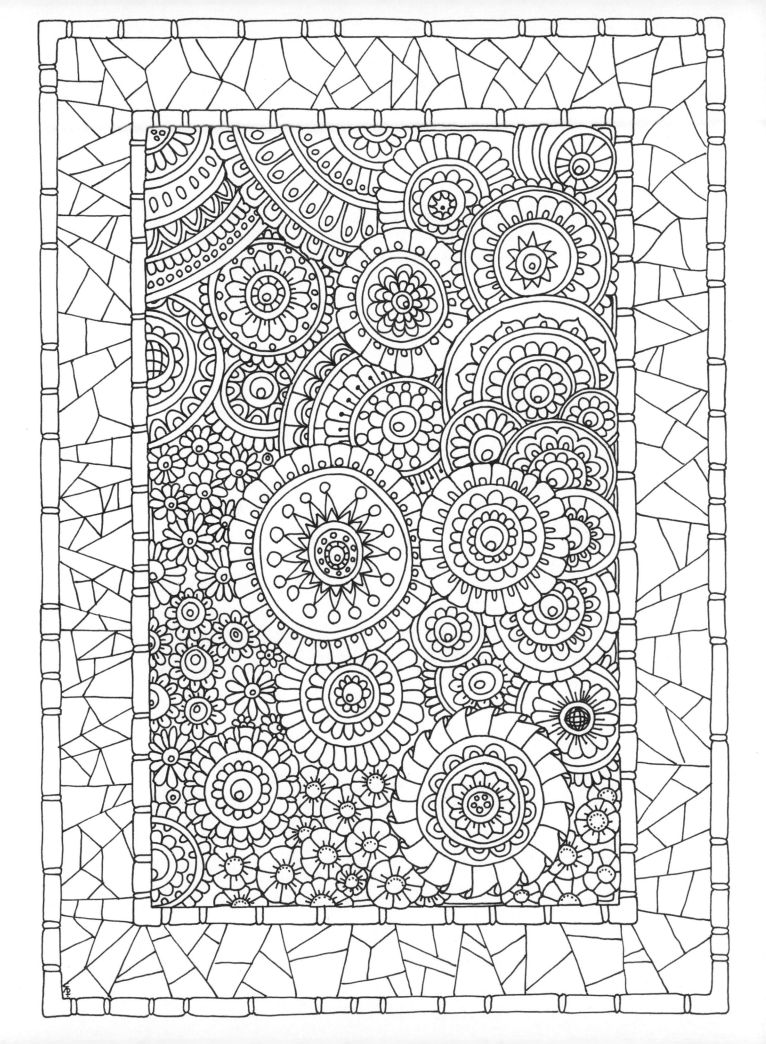

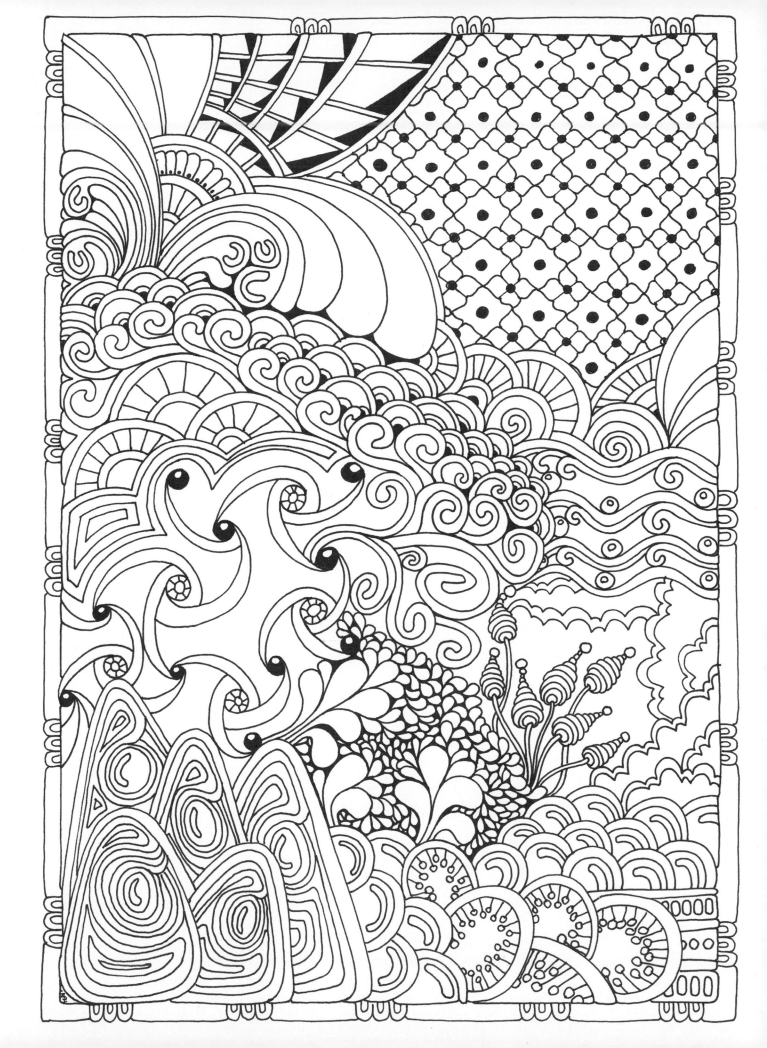

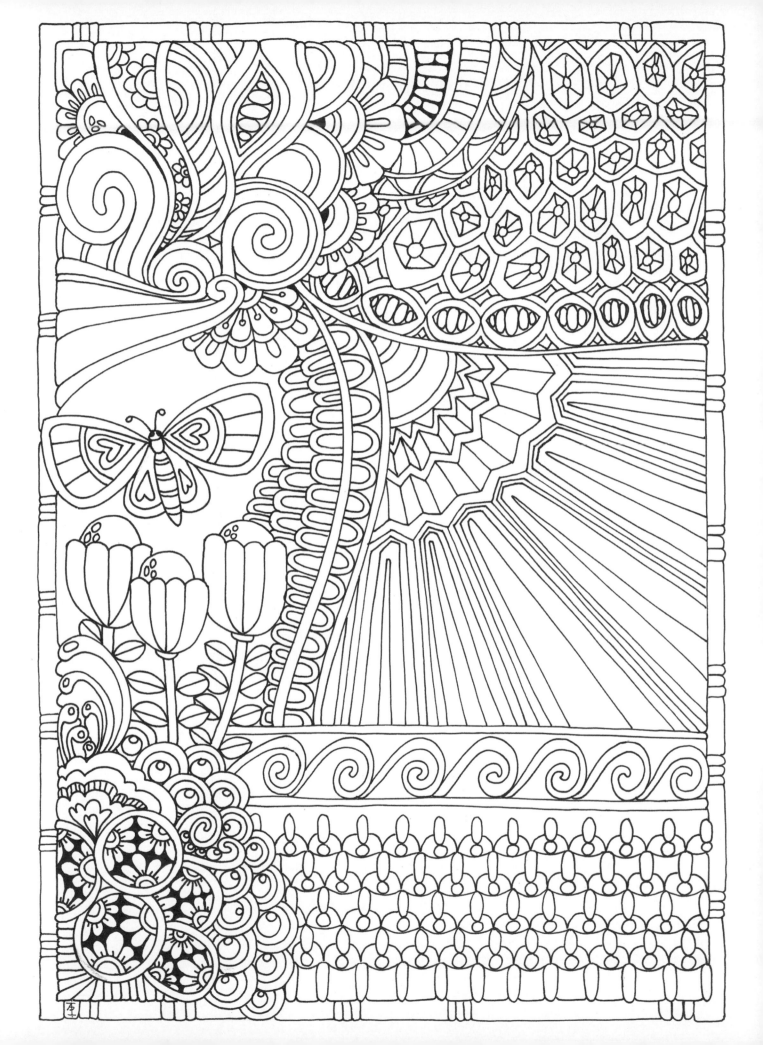

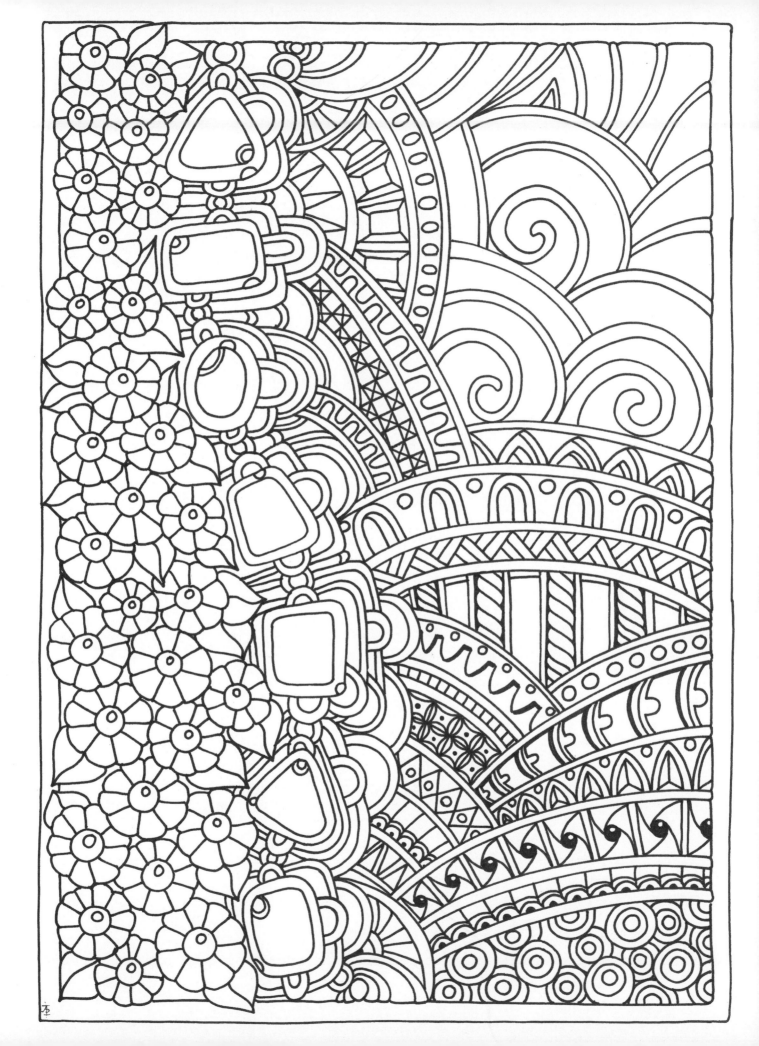

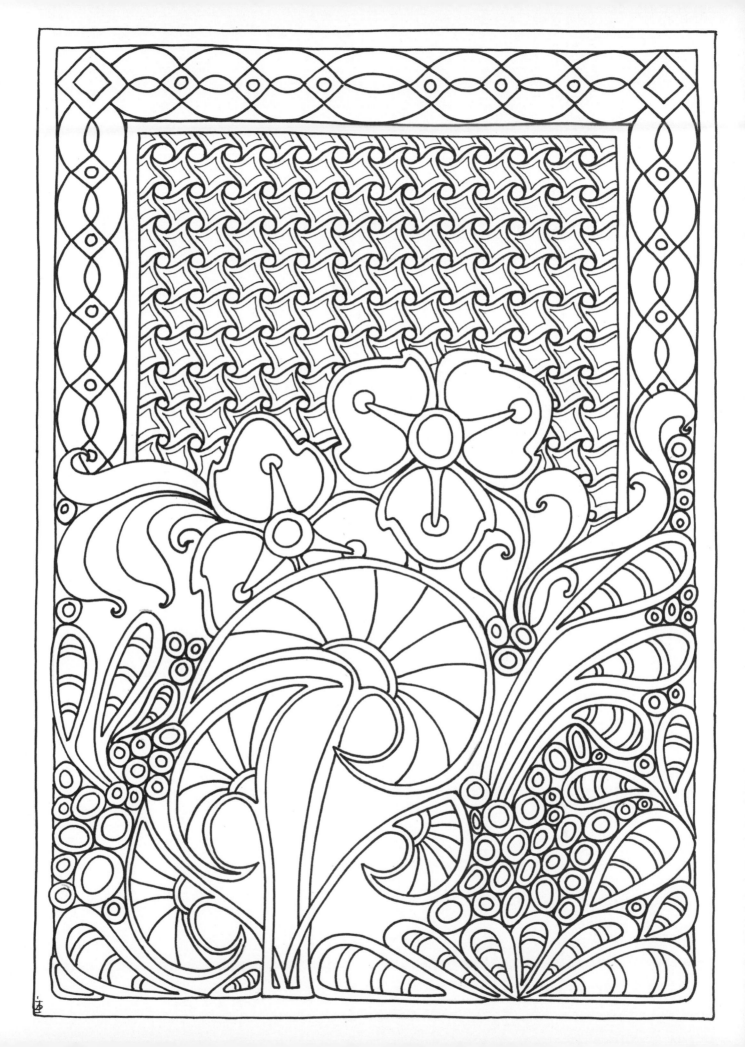

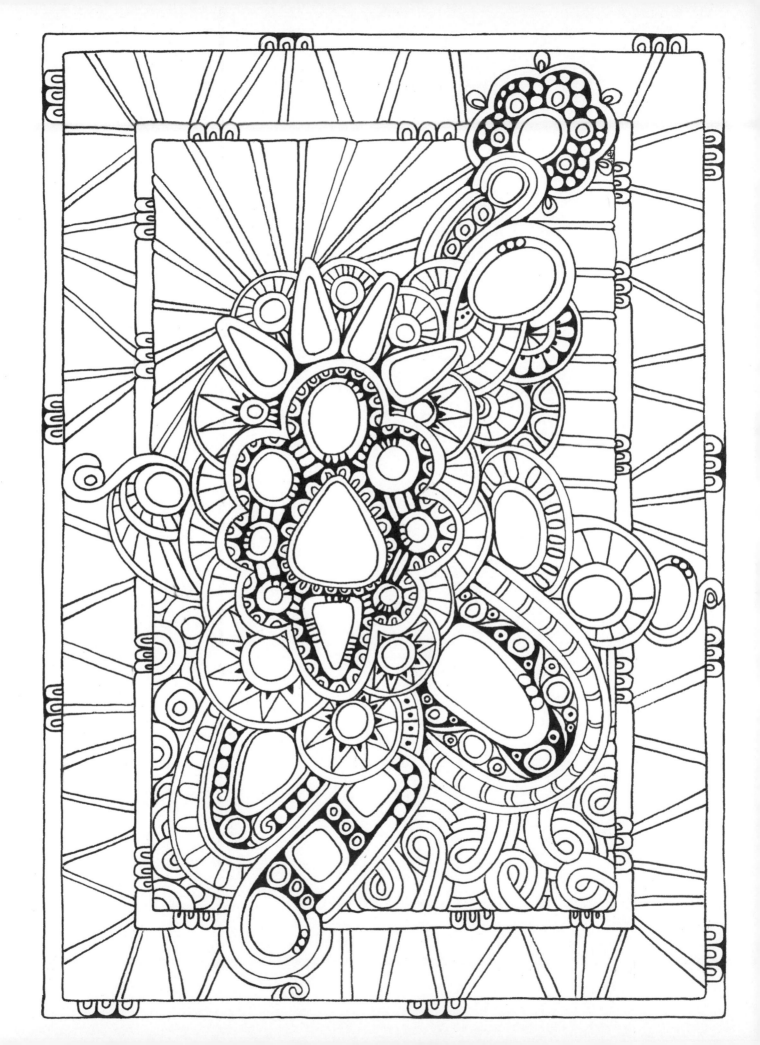

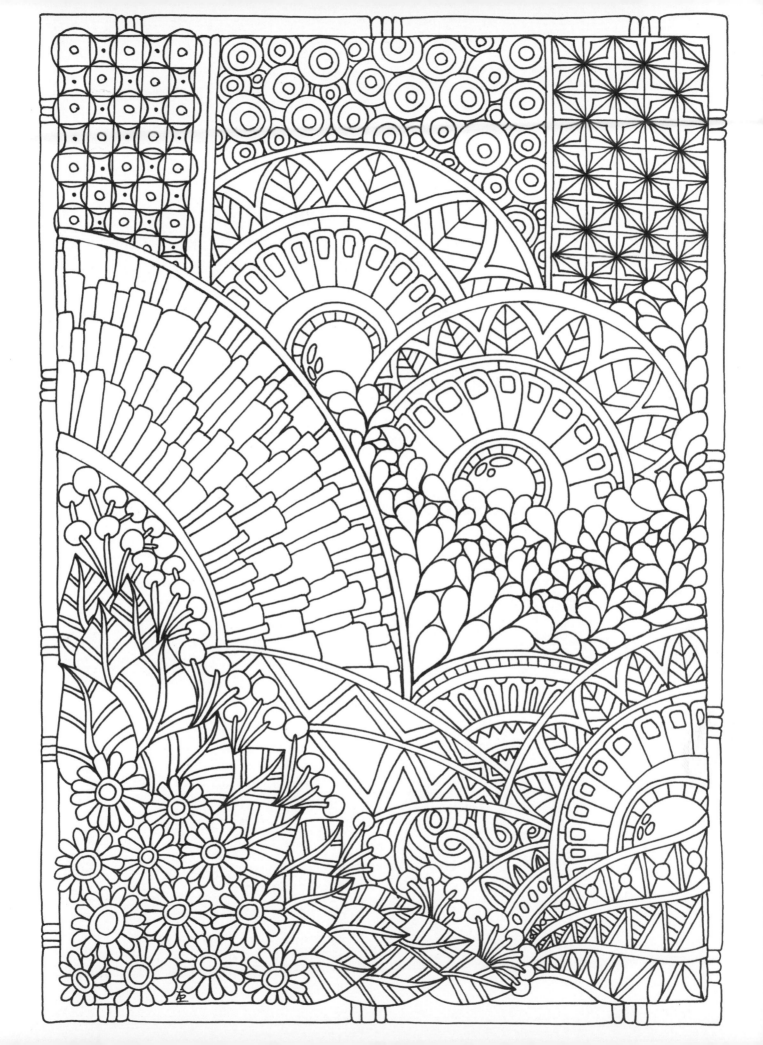

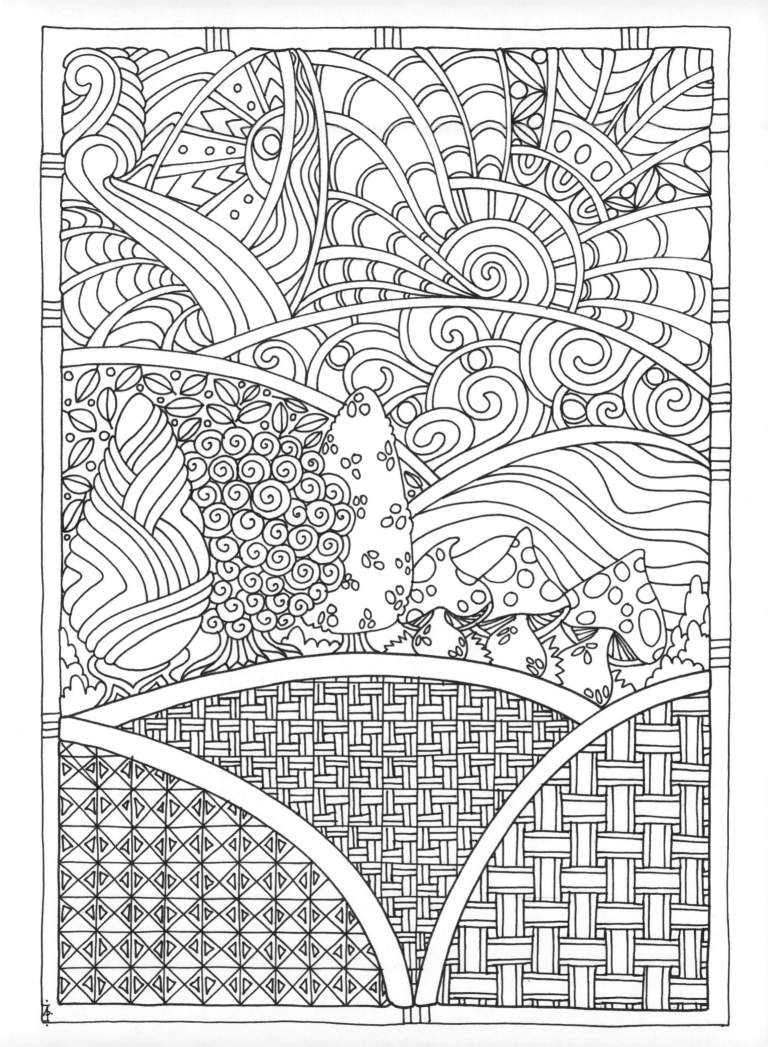

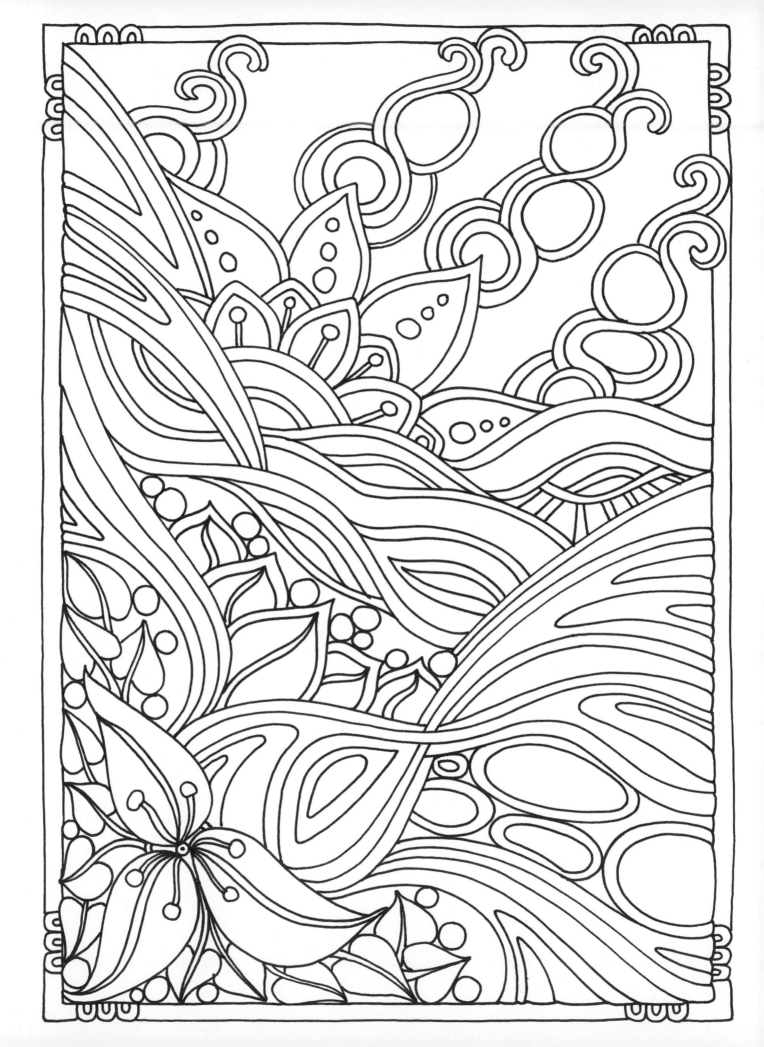

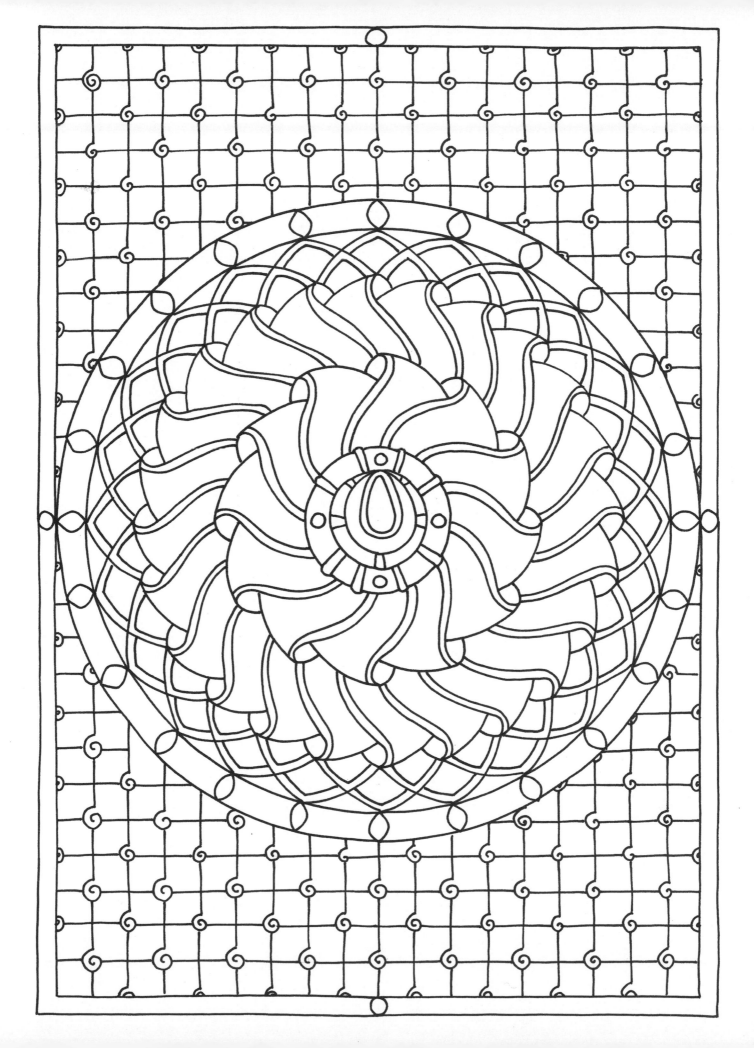

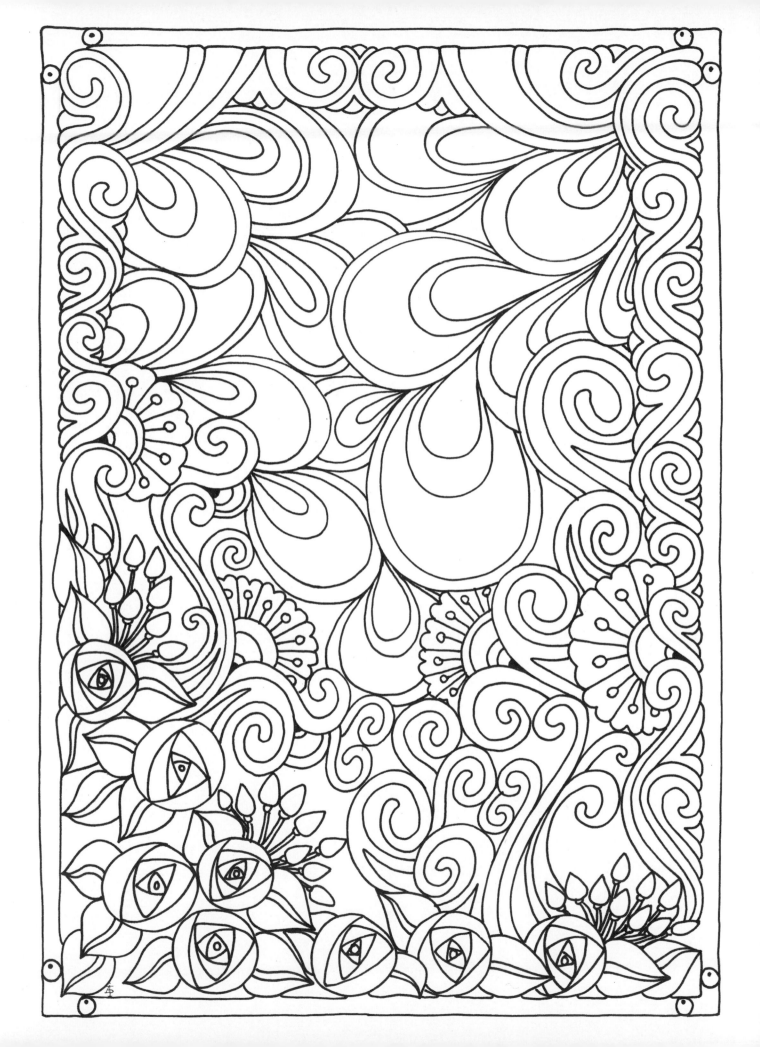

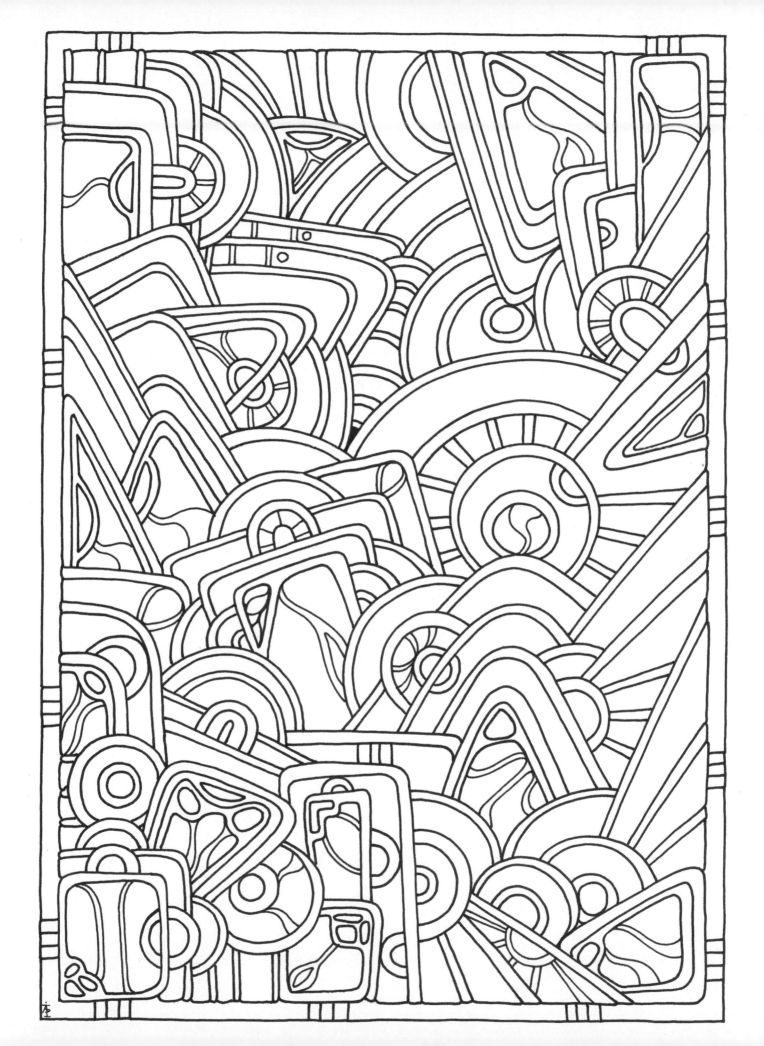

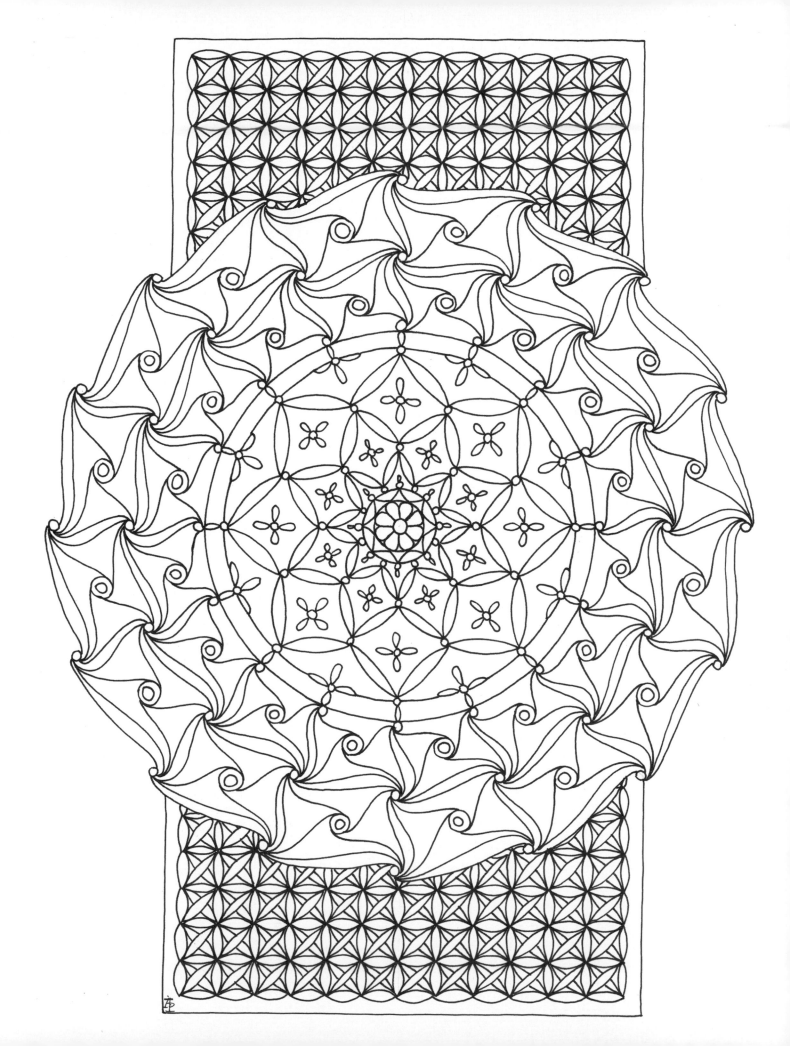

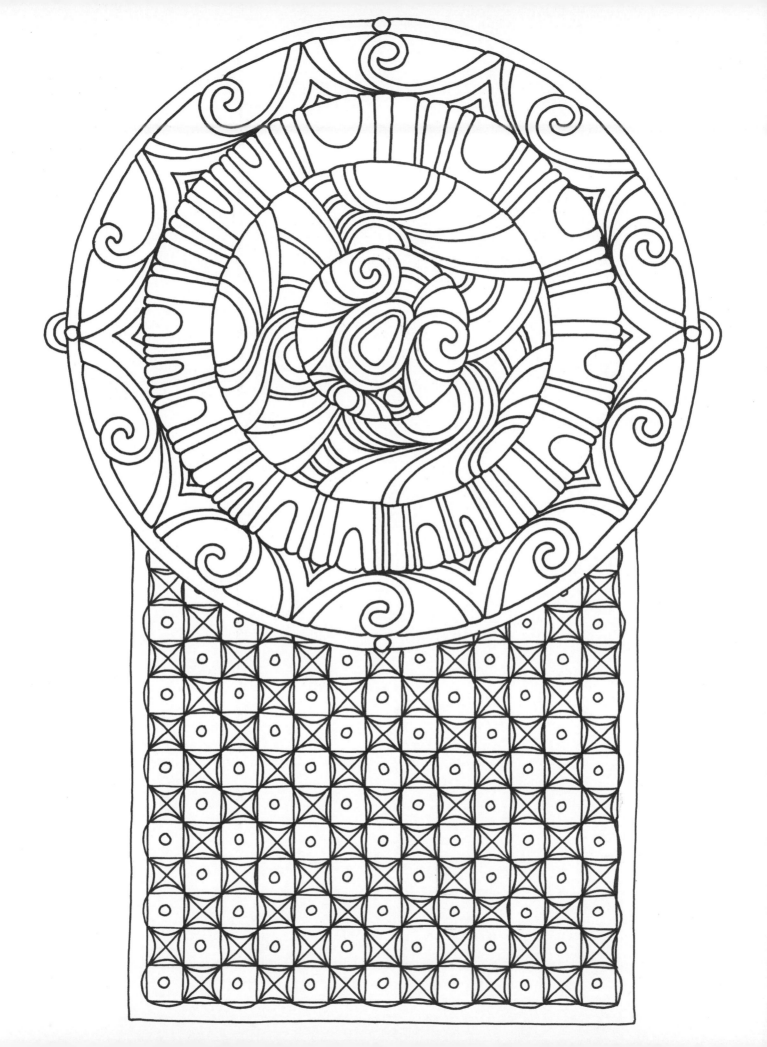

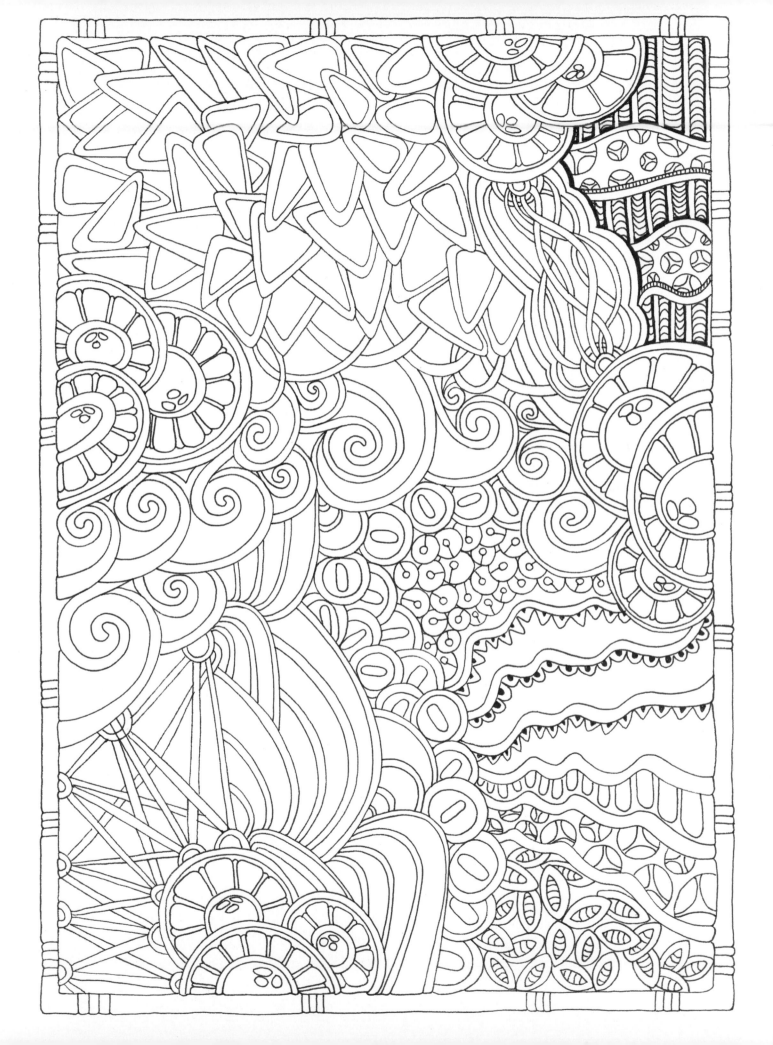

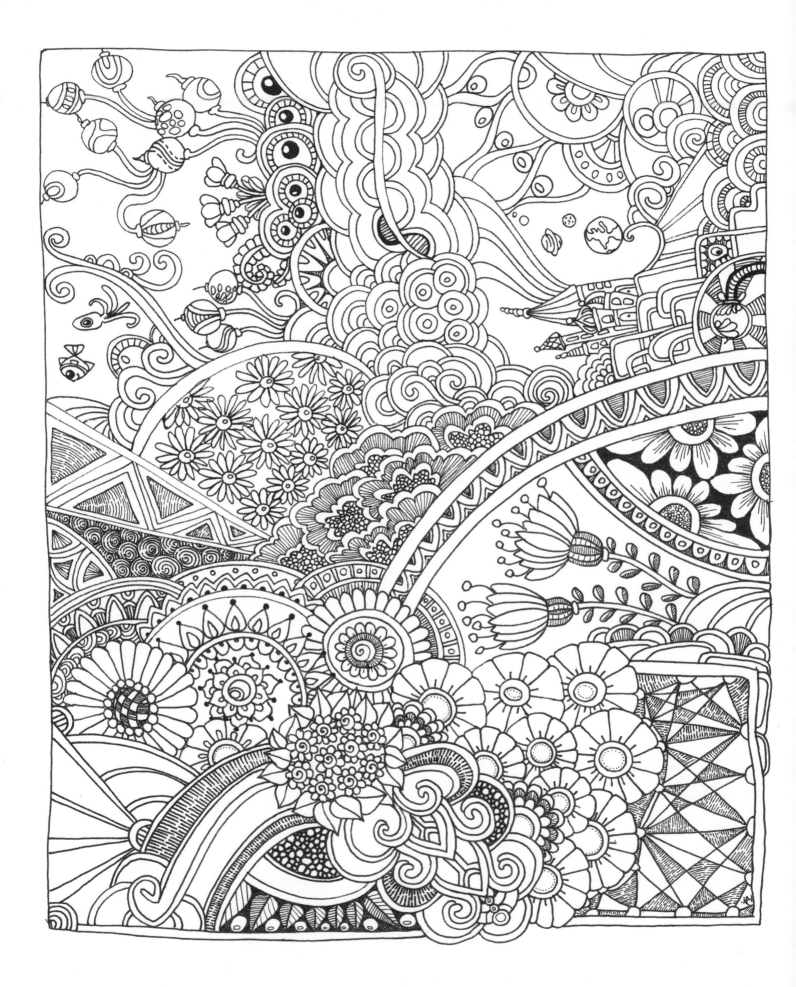

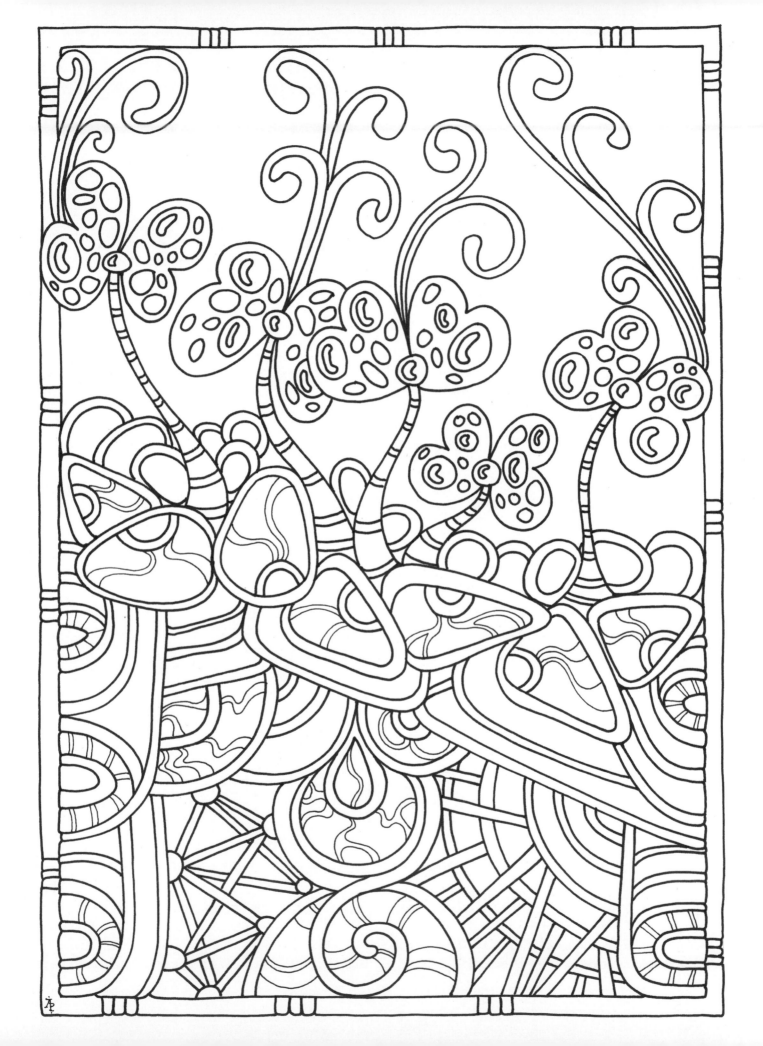

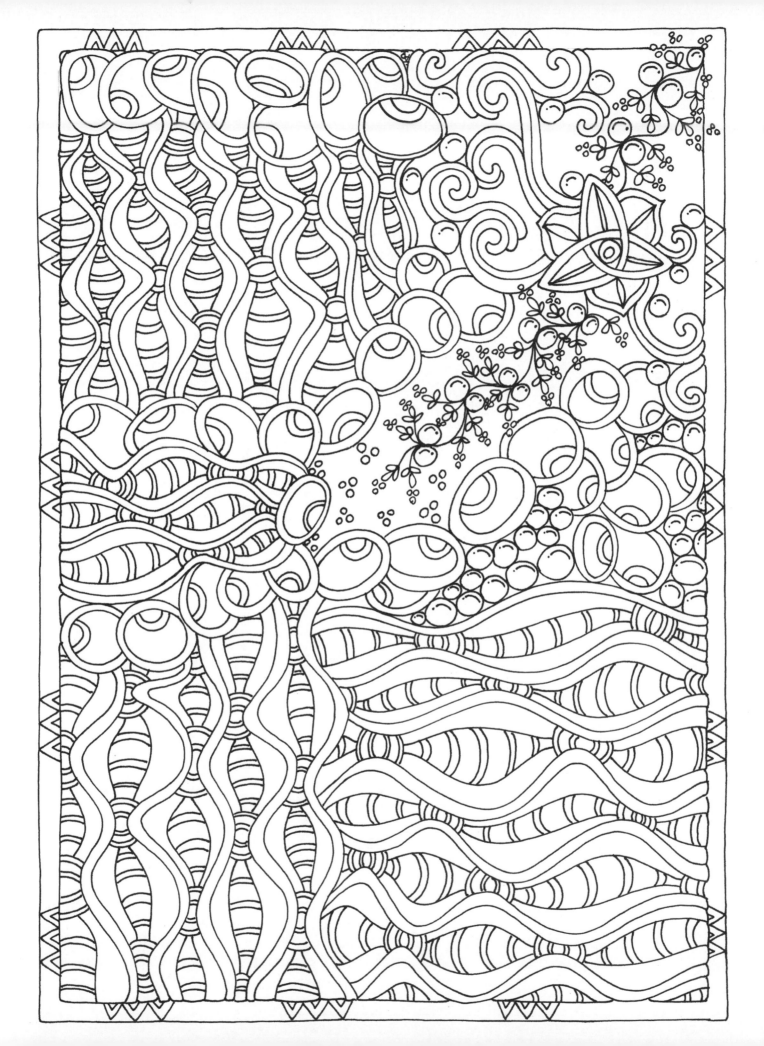

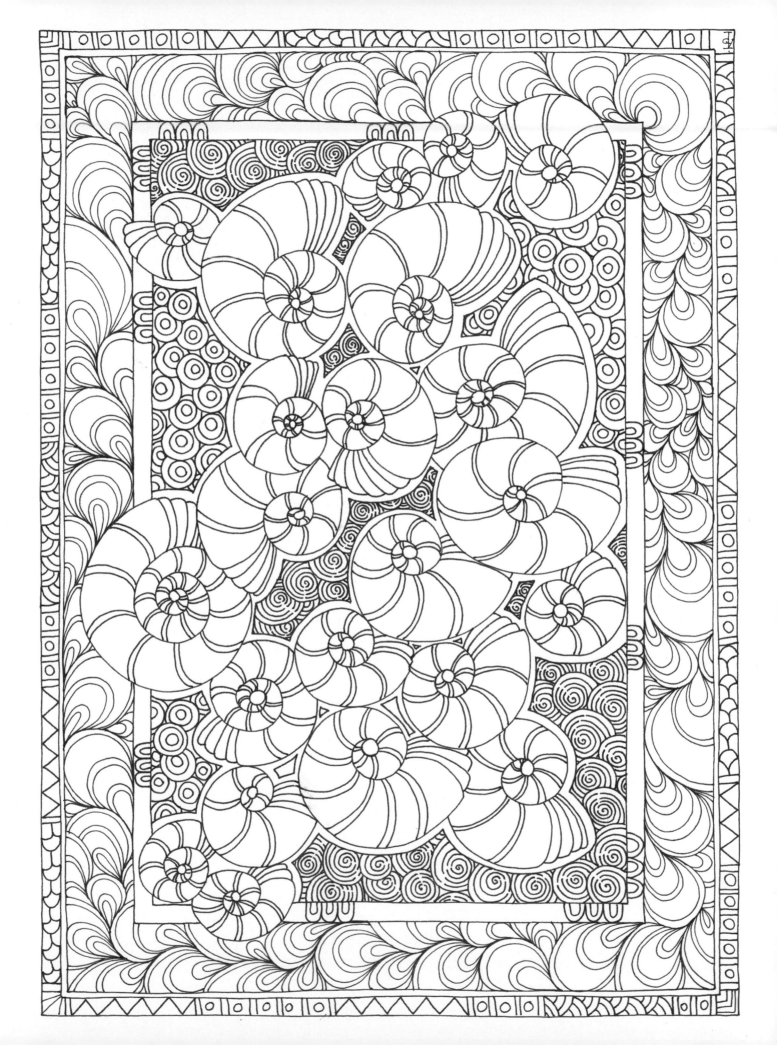

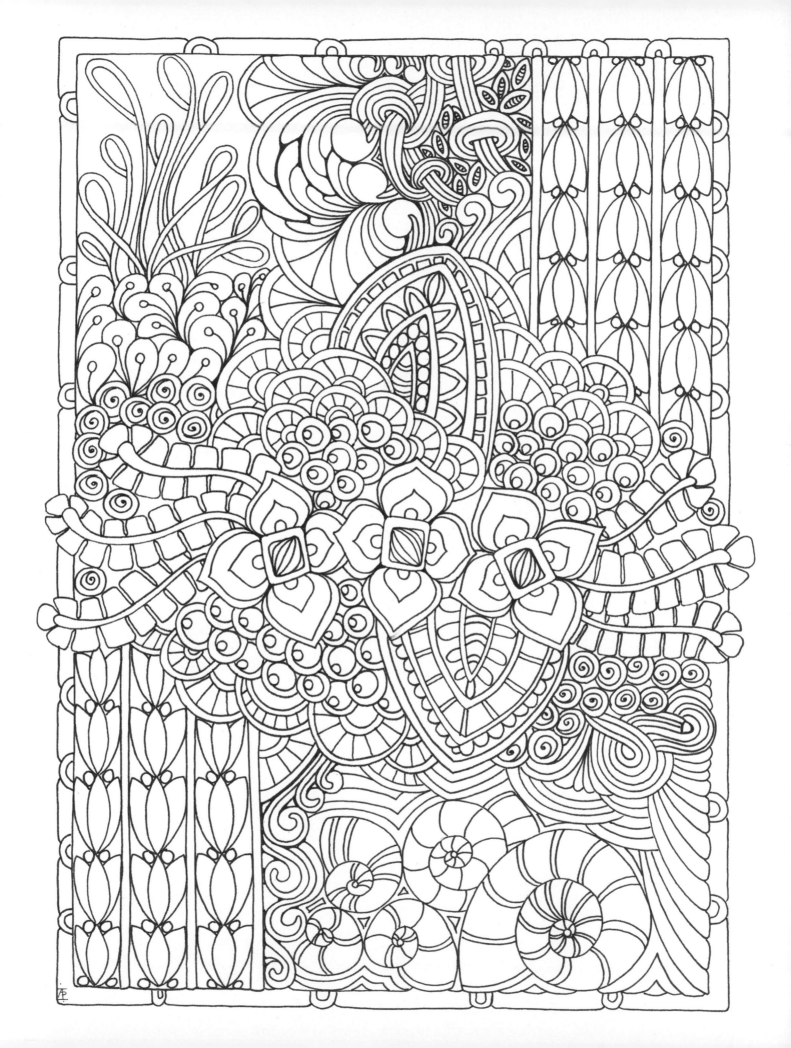

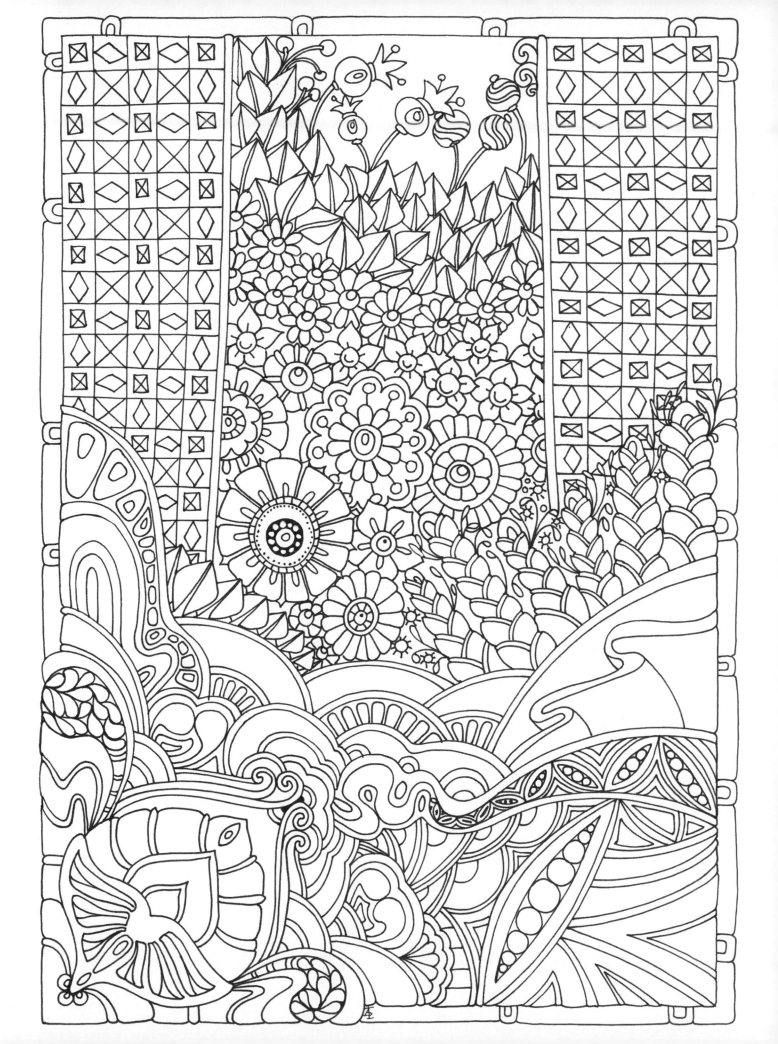

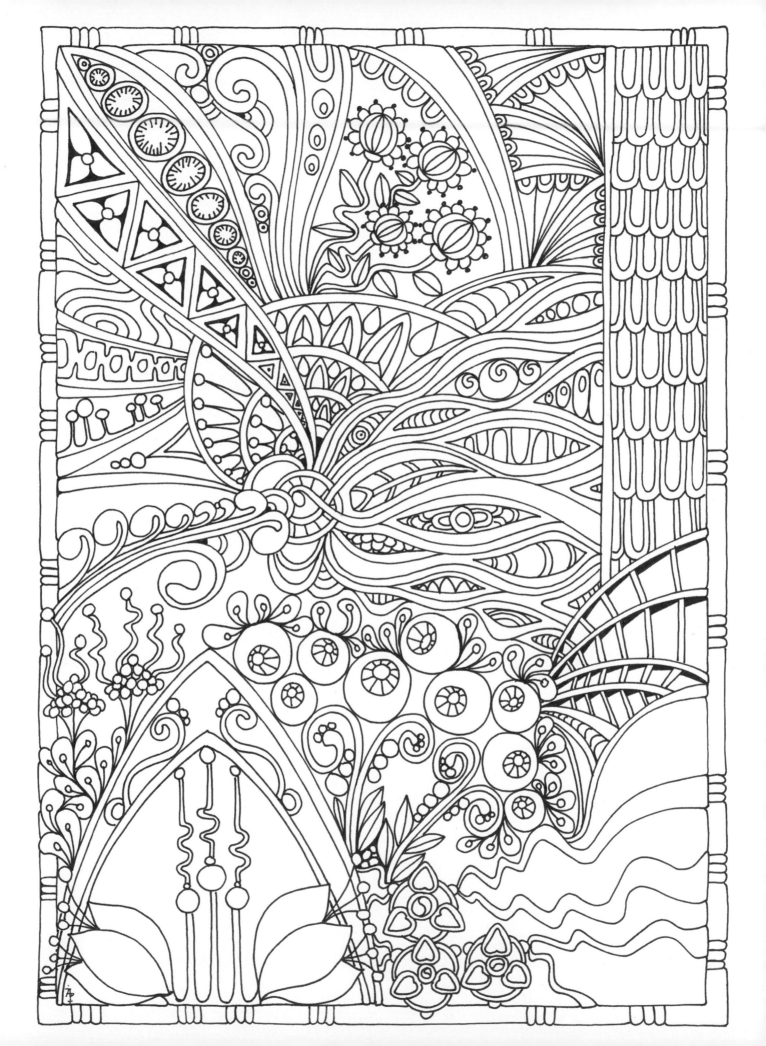

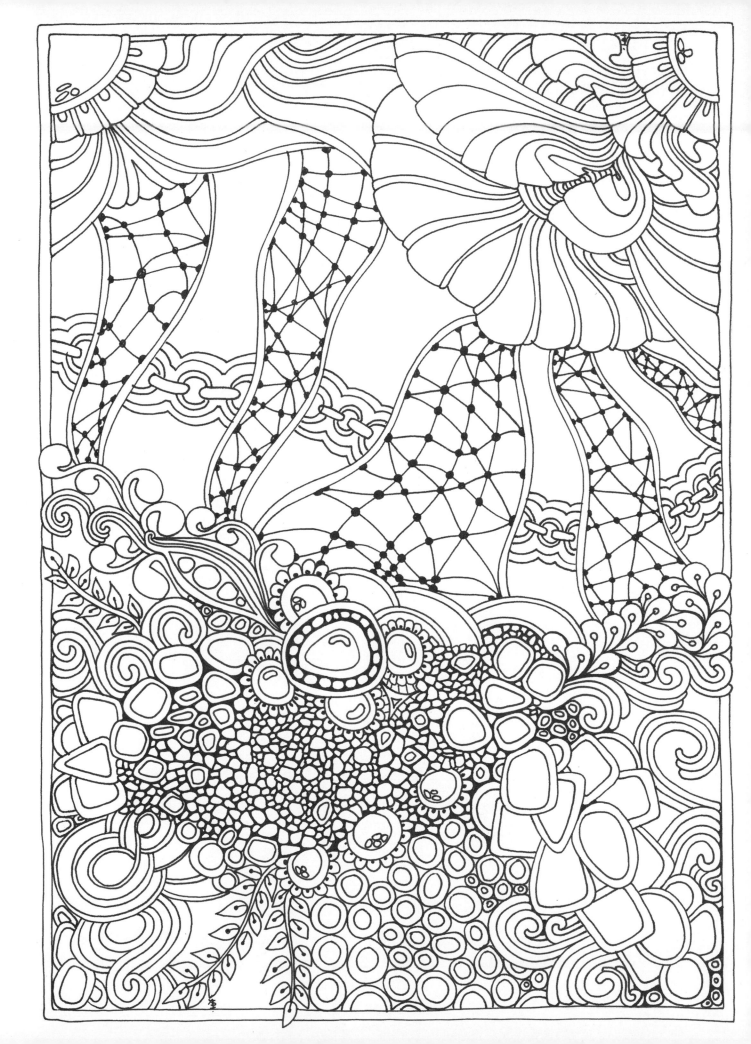

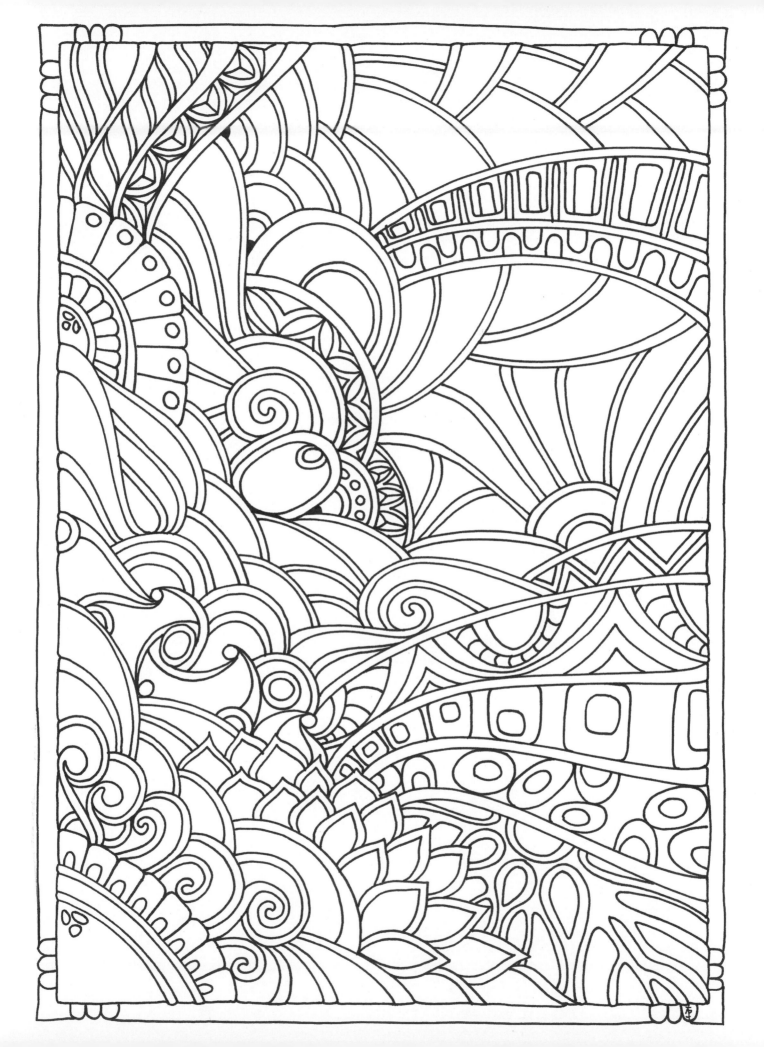

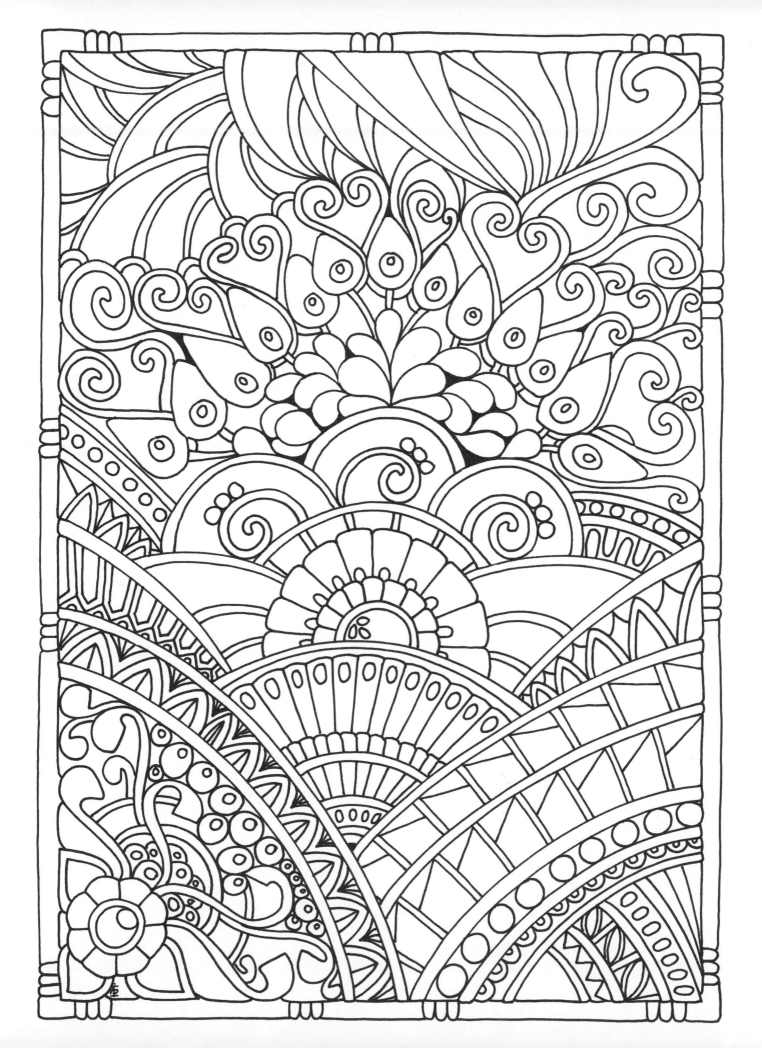

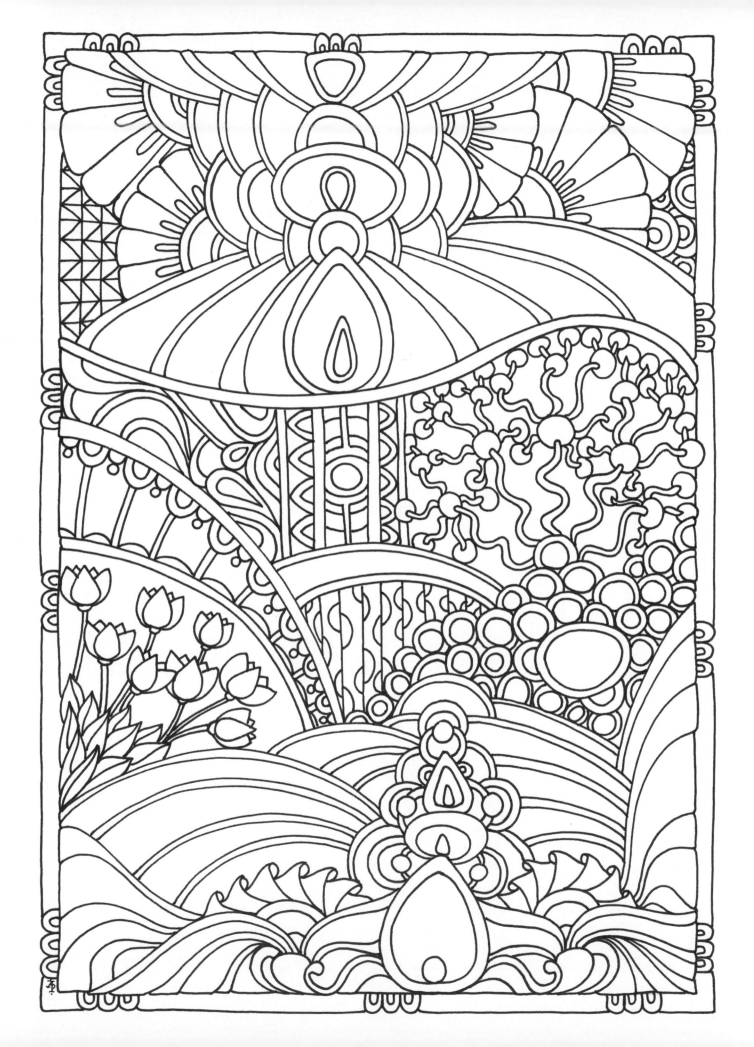

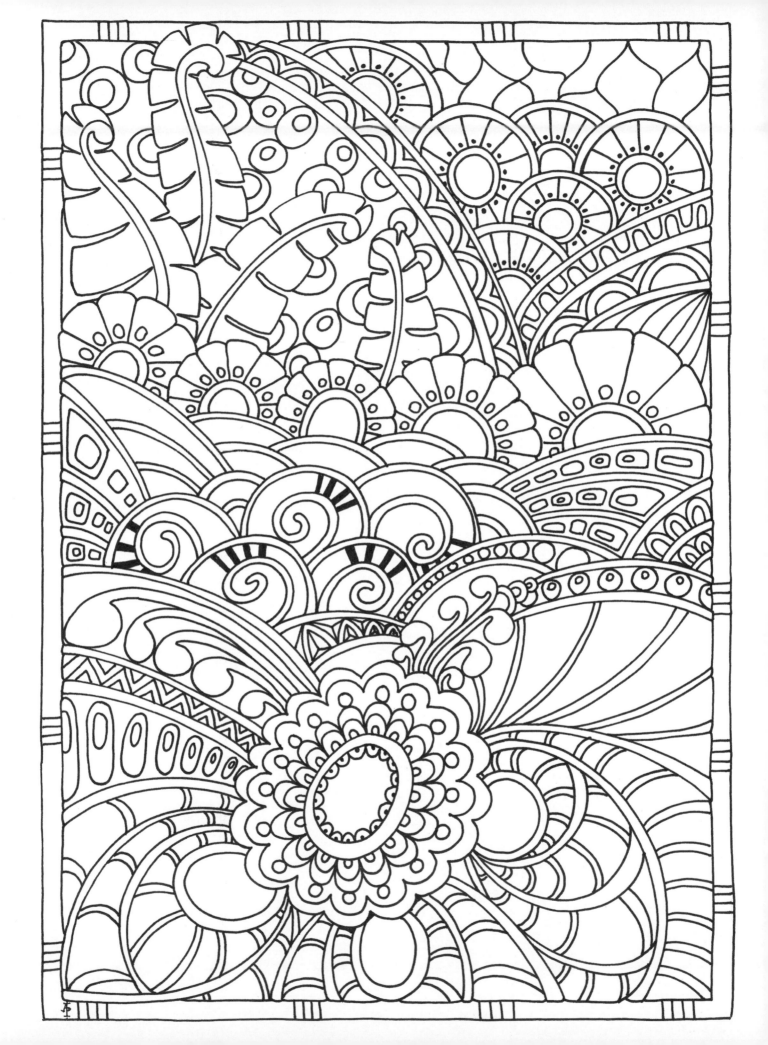

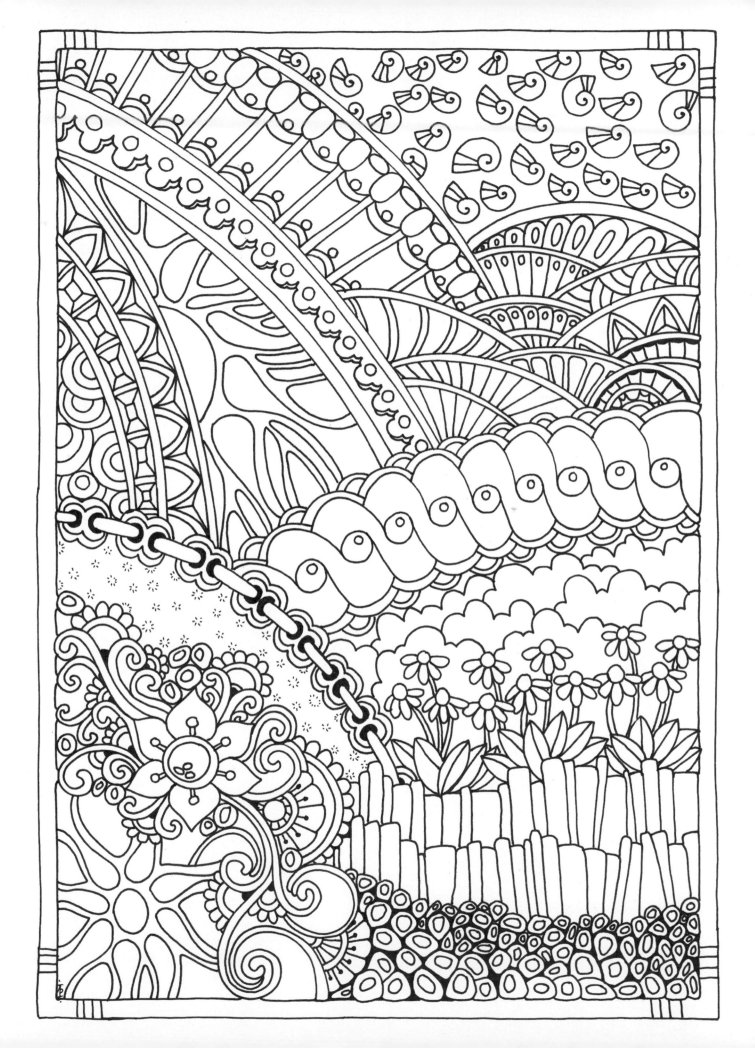

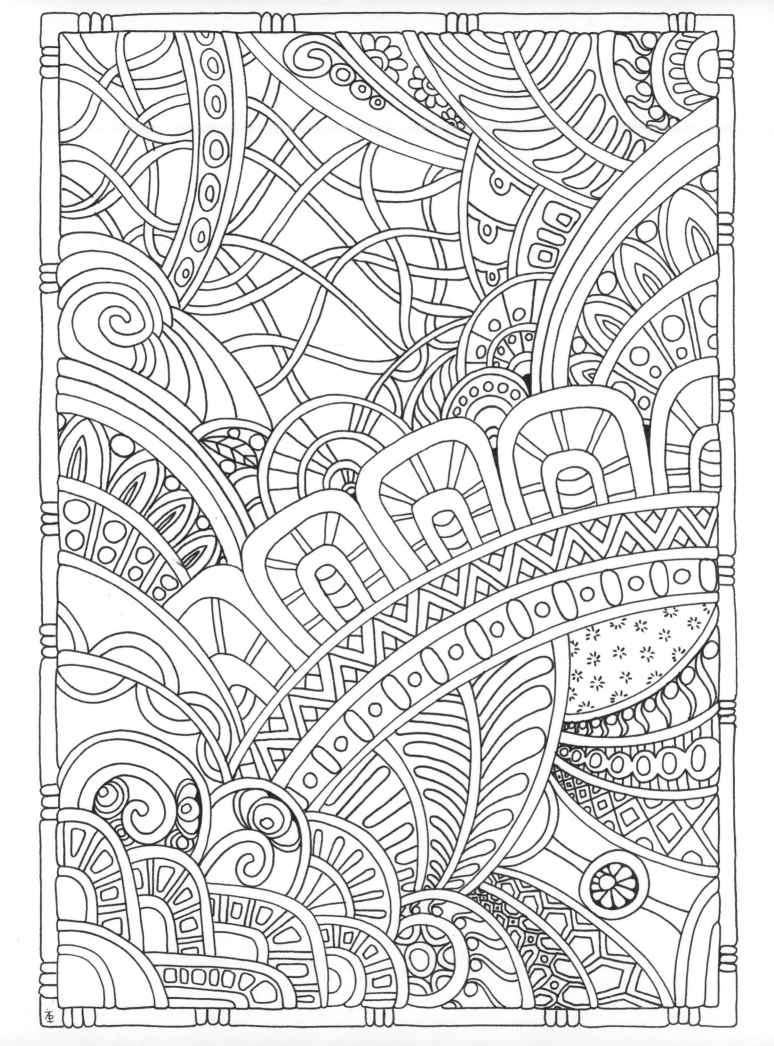

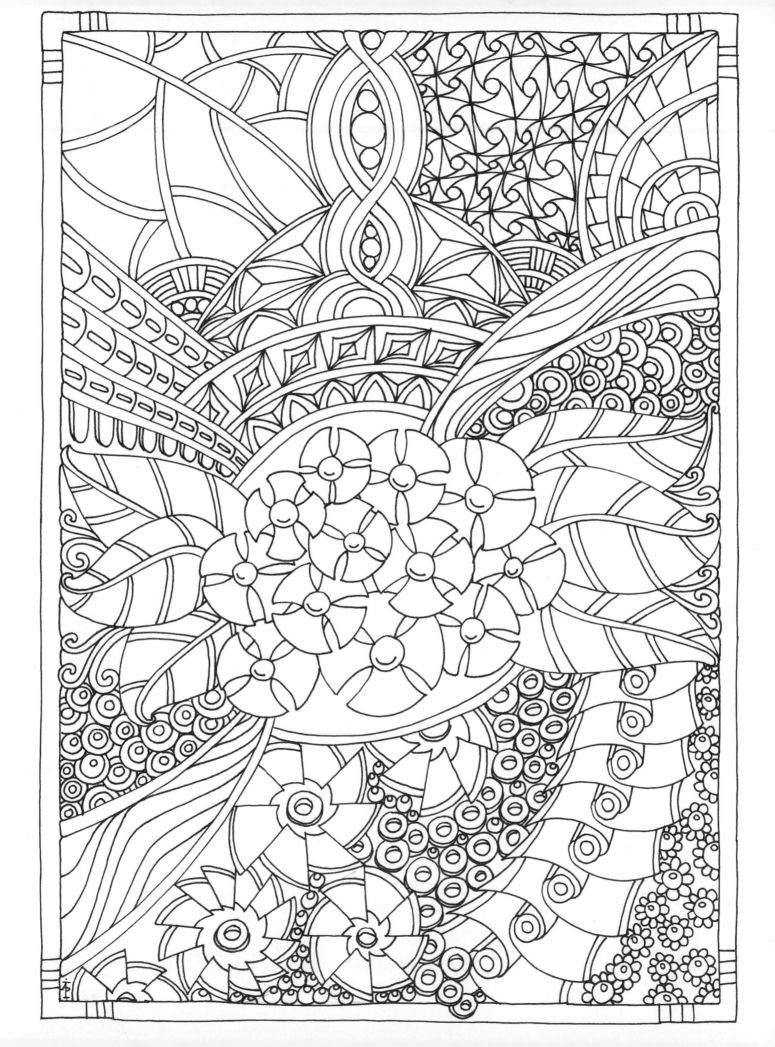

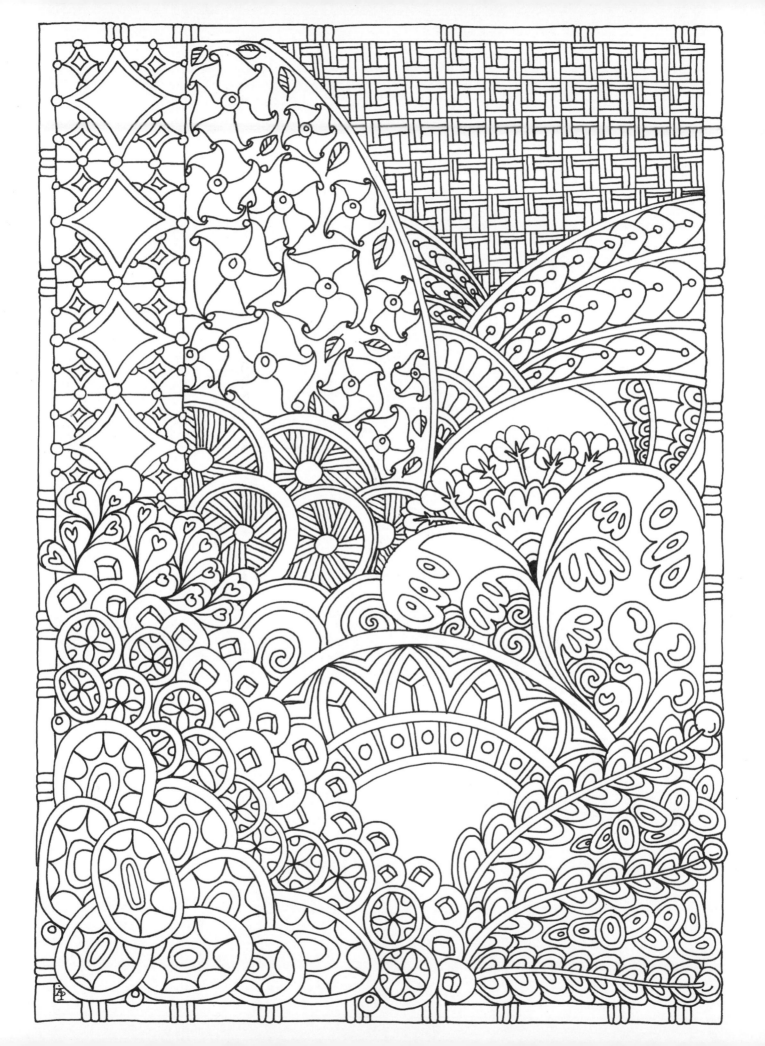

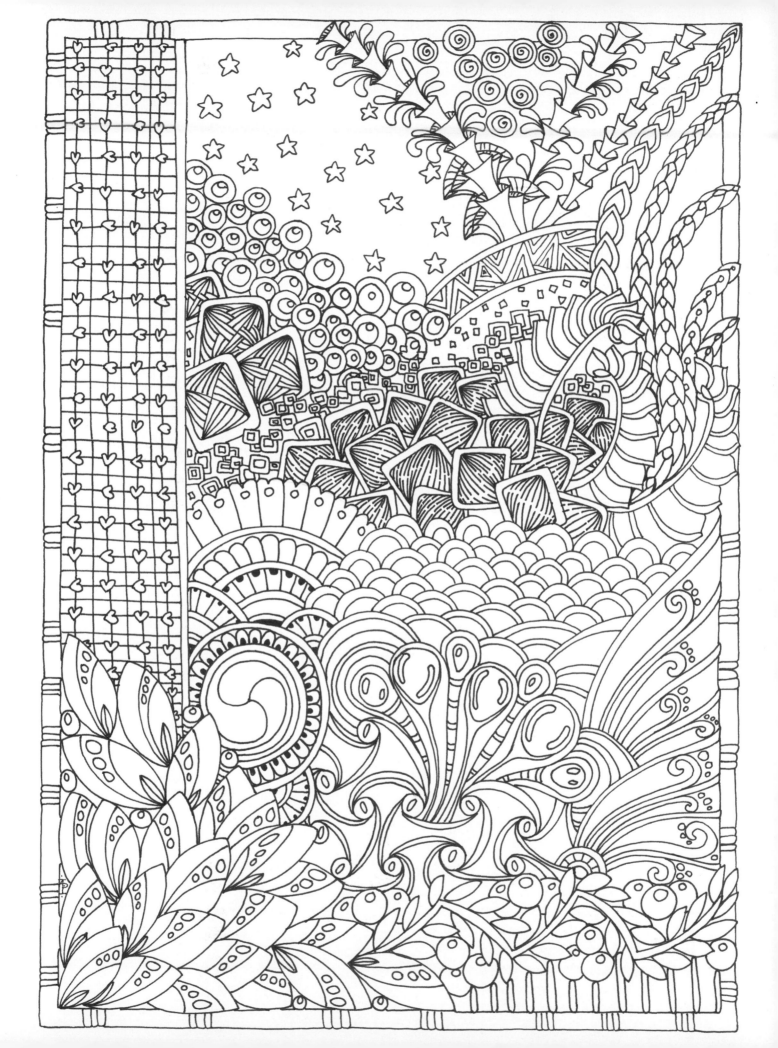

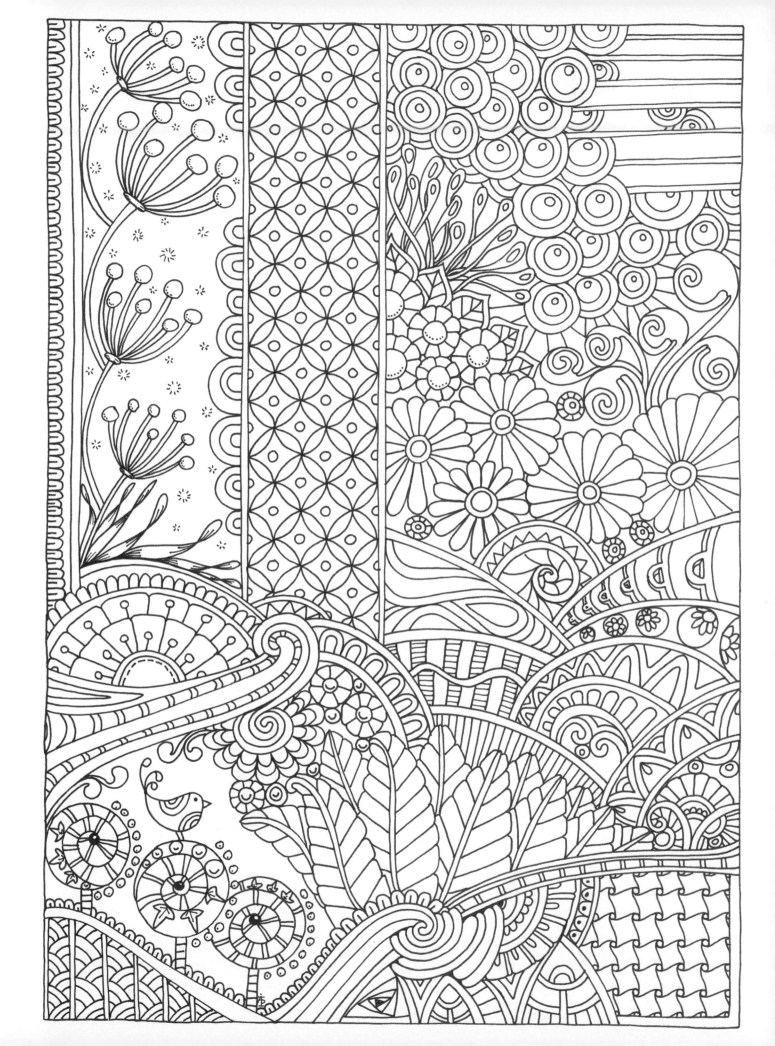

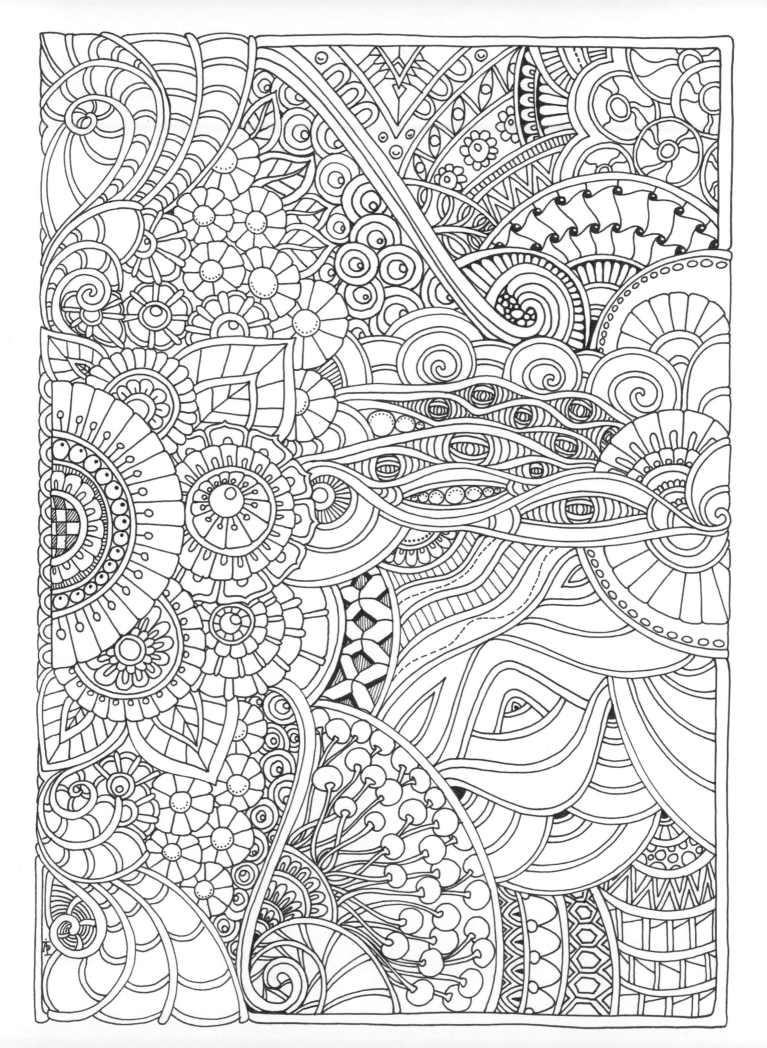

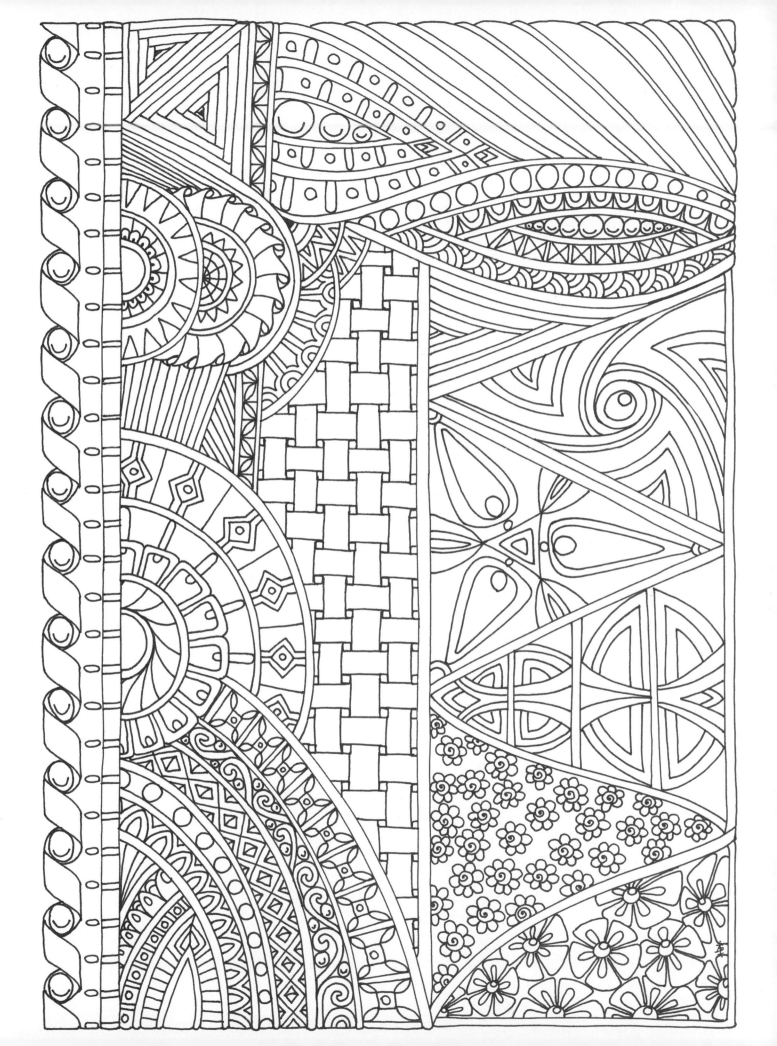

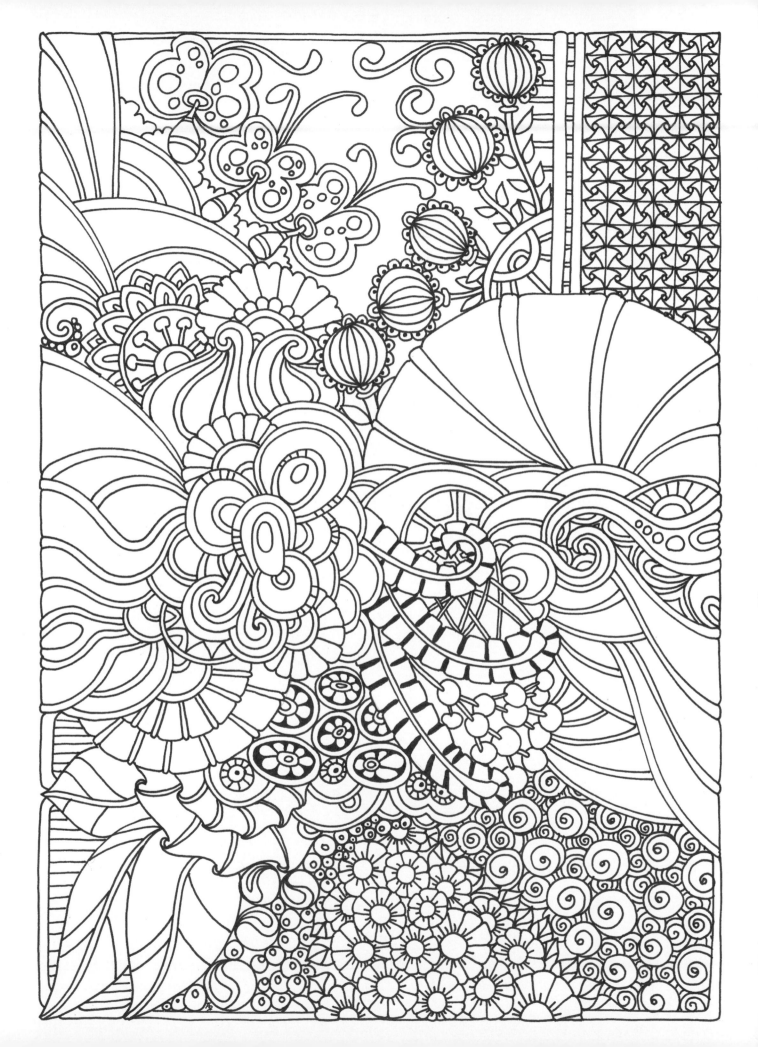

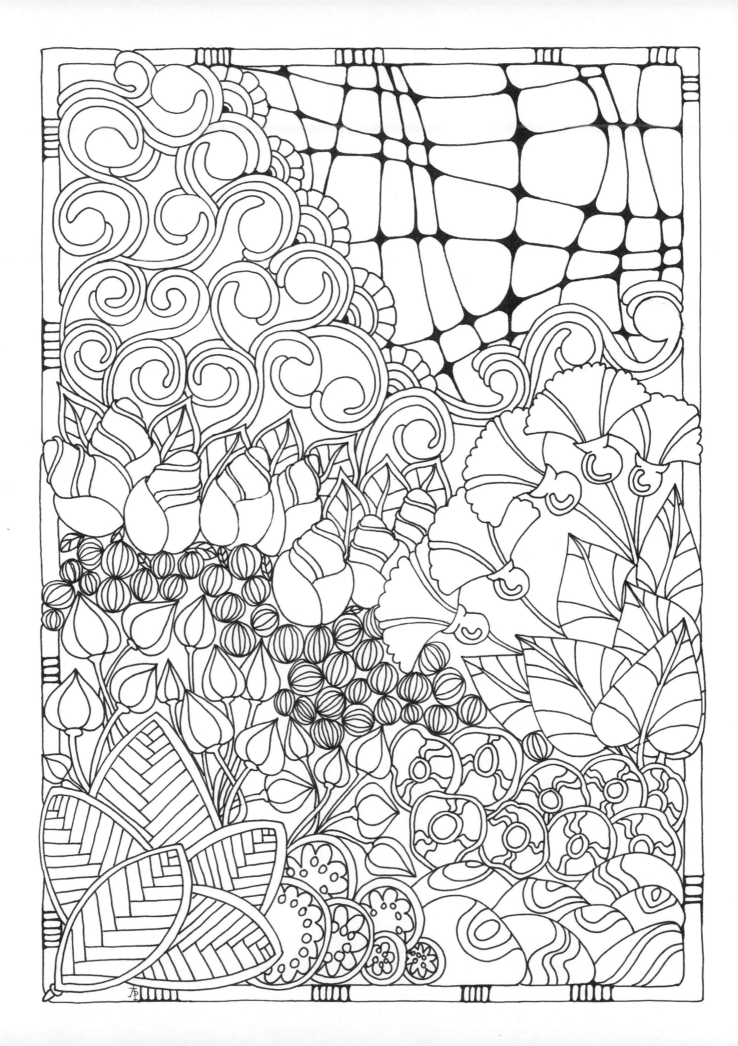

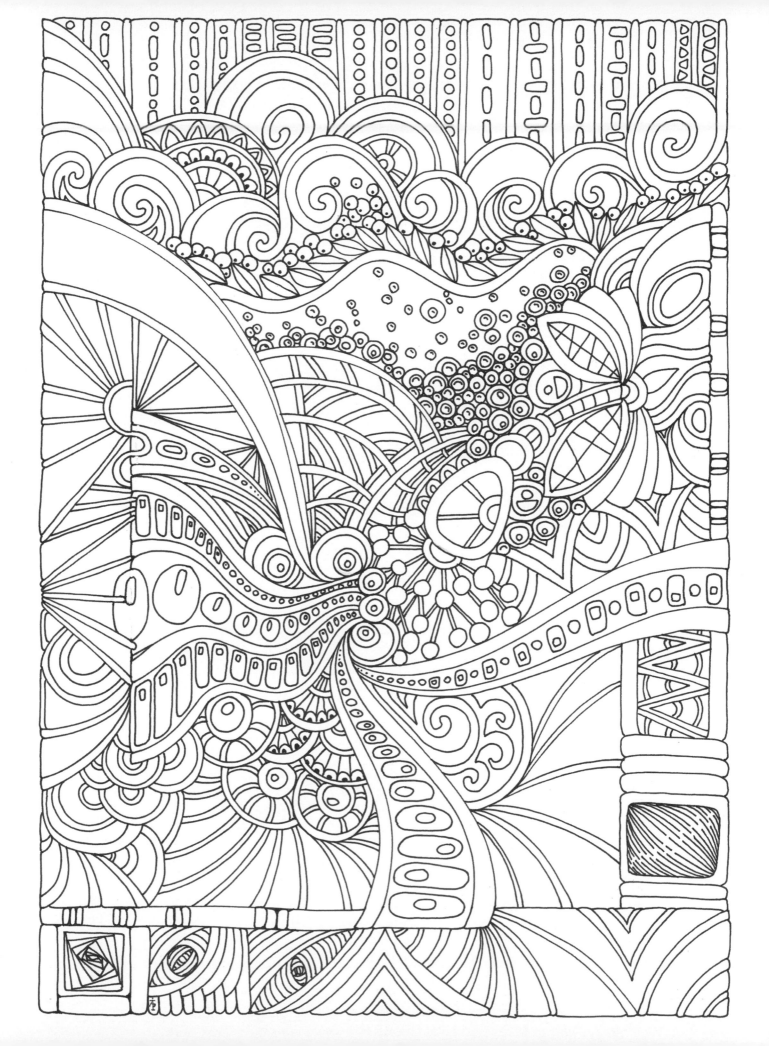

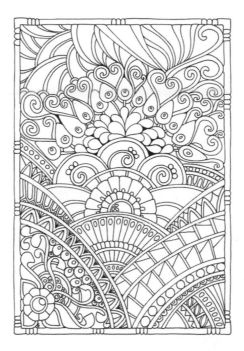

Zen doodling emerged in the early nineties within the field of art therapy. With its repetitive patterns and expressive qualities, Zen doodling aids stressed colorists in focus and mindfulness. The form consists of all different types of patterns and motifs—free-form swirling, circular, and geometric sequences woven together and built upon one another—that relax colorists and enable them to express their creativity.

Recently, Zen doodling made its way into the adult coloring book world and has been helping colorists unwind ever since. *Angela Porter's Zen Doodle Designs* mimics and embraces the Zen doodle style in both the creation of the designs and the coloring of the illustrations—only the latter is up to you!

These beautiful and intricate outlines incorporate Porter's own unique and intuitive style. Her illustrations are drawn completely by hand and often contain imperfections, giving the designs a human aspect that is highly sought after by many colorists. Additionally, her style includes thick, bold lines that flow with ease and tranquility, making them perfect for de-stressing as you color.

∽

Angela Porter is a *New York Times* bestselling illustrator and a self-taught artist. She finds inspiration in the architecture, archaeology, industrial and scientific heritage, and nature of her surroundings. Much of her intricate work is abstract and whimsical with imaginative elements, rich with flowing lines that create textured and detailed designs. A special-needs science teacher for more than twenty-seven years, Angela relaxes with her art and also by playing the flute and learning to play electric folk harp. She lives in South Wales, Great Britain, with her crazy white cat that has a fondness for a nice warm mug of tea.

Also Available from Skyhorse Publishing

Creative Stress Relieving Adult Coloring Book Series

Art Nouveau: Coloring for Artists
Art Nouveau: Coloring for Everyone
Curious Cats and Kittens: Coloring for Artists
Curious Cats and Kittens: Coloring for Everyone
Mandalas: Coloring for Artists
Mandalas: Coloring for Everyone
Mehndi: Coloring for Artists
Mehndi: Coloring for Everyone
Nirvana: Coloring for Artists
Nirvana: Coloring for Everyone

Paisleys: Coloring for Artists
Paisleys: Coloring for Everyone
Tapestries, Fabrics, and Quilts: Coloring for Artists
Tapestries, Fabrics, and Quilts: Coloring for Everyone
Whimsical Designs: Coloring for Artists
Whimsical Designs: Coloring for Everyone
Whimsical Woodland Creatures: Coloring for Everyone
Zen Patterns and Designs: Coloring for Artists
Zen Patterns and Designs: Coloring for Everyone

New York Times Bestselling Artists' Adult Coloring Book Series

Alberta Hutchinson's Instant Zen Designs: New York Times *Bestselling Artists' Adult Coloring Books*
Alberta Hutchinson's Peace Mandalas: New York Times *Bestselling Artists' Adult Coloring Books*
Marjorie Sarnat's Fanciful Fashions: New York Times *Bestselling Artists' Adult Coloring Books*
Marjorie Sarnat's Pampered Pets: New York Times *Bestselling Artists' Adult Coloring Books*
Marty Noble's Sugar Skulls: New York Times *Bestselling Artists' Adult Coloring Books*
Marty Noble's Peaceful World: New York Times *Bestselling Artists' Adult Coloring Books*

The Peaceful Adult Coloring Book Series

Adult Coloring Book: Be Inspired
Adult Coloring Book: De-Stress
Adult Coloring Book: Keep Calm
Adult Coloring Book: Relax

Portable Coloring for Creative Adults

Calming Patterns: Portable Coloring for Creative Adults
Flying Wonders: Portable Coloring for Creative Adults
Natural Wonders: Portable Coloring for Creative Adults
Sea Life: Portable Coloring for Creative Adults